HOWARD BARKER'S
THEATRE OF SEDUCTION

Contemporary Theatre Studies

A series of books edited by Franc Chamberlain, Nene College, Northampton, UK

Please see the back of this book for other titles in the Contemporary Theatre Studies series

HOWARD BARKER'S
THEATRE OF SEDUCTION

Charles Lamb

*Bournemouth and Poole College of Further Education,
Dorset, UK*

 harwood academic publishers
Australia • Canada • China • France • Germany • India
Japan • Luxembourg • Malaysia • The Netherlands • Russia
Singapore • Switzerland • Thailand • United Kingdom

Copyright © 1997 OPA (Overseas Publishers Association) Amsterdam B.V.
Published in the Netherlands by Harwood Academic Publishers.

Amsteldijk 166
1st Floor
1079 LH Amsterdam
The Netherlands

British Library Cataloguing in Publication Data
Lamb, Charles
    Howard Barker's theatre of seduction. – (Contemporary
theatre studies; v. 19)
    1. Barker, Howard, 1946 – Criticism and interpretation
    2. Dramatists, English – 20th century
    3. English drama – 20th century – History and criticism
    I. Title
    822.9'14

    ISBN 3-7186-5884-4

Cover illustration: 'Put this on, please …' *The Castle*, Act I, Scene 1.

CONTENTS

INTRODUCTION TO THE SERIES

Contemporary Theatre Studies is a book series of special interest to everyone involved in theatre. It consists of monographs on influential figures, studies of movements and ideas in theatre, as well as primary material consisting of theatre-related documents, performing editions of plays in English, and English translations of plays from various vital theatre traditions worldwide.

Franc Chamberlain

LIST OF PLATES

1. The home-coming of the Crusaders. *The Castle*, Act I, Scene 1.
2. 'Put this on, please …' *The Castle*, Act I, Scene 1.
3. *The Castle*.
4. The trial of Skinner. *The Castle*, Act II, Scene 2.
5. 'There is one …' *The Castle*, Act II, Scene 3.
6. 'Don't draw cunt, I'm talking …' *The Castle*, Act II, Scene 4.
7. 'Raining women … ' *The Castle*, Act II, Scene 5.
8. 'All women big about the middle, lock up … ' *The Castle*, Act II, Scene 5.
9. 'No, you govern it instead … ' *The Castle*, Act II, Scene 6.

PREFACE

My point of departure for this study took the form of a practical problem: none of the contemporary performance theory that I knew was of any real use whatsoever or provided the least assistance in staging Howard Barker's plays. This conclusion was based on my own experience of directing and acting in Barker plays as well as a wide acquaintanceship with major professional productions of his work. I felt somehow that the full dramatic potential, especially of the later texts, was not being realised in performance. On the other hand there was throughout the sixties, seventies and eighties an unprecedented interest in and awareness of theatre as theatre: theatrical performance was no longer seen as a simple 'fleshing out' of the dramatic text but rather as a craft in its own right quite separate from literary fiction and from film. This period witnessed the widespread dissemination of Theatre Studies in Universities and Colleges, while in schools drama was established as an independent subject within the curriculum. There was, consequently, a considerable new interest in theoretical approaches to performance.

Barker, however, seemed to be increasingly at odds with the current theatrical climate of the seventies and eighties. He appeared to be pursuing a more classical and perhaps more conservative aesthetic — though his plays did not demonstrate the 'accessibility' that such an approach might suggest; on the contrary they became increasingly 'difficult'. There is a sense now that directors have very little idea of how to 'cope' with these texts. I think this is in no small measure owing to the lack of any kind of theoretical basis on which to proceed with them. My starting point for this exploration was the problem — the challenge — that Barker's plays posed to contemporary performance theory.

While working on this study, I was fortunate in being permitted to observe rehearsals of professional productions of Barker's plays. It was at one of these — during the RSC's work on *The Bite of the Night* — that I devised the strategy which informs this study. The director was having difficulty working on some scenes in the third act and I noticed that a consistent pattern was emerging. A scene would be built up logically, with a pattern of clear and consistent motivations. At a certain point, however, an action would occur which violently broke with the foregoing 'rationale'. Discussion between actors and director yielded no more than that this was an 'irrational' moment. Whereupon the action was proceeded with along the same lines as before, i.e. every effort was made to put the previous 'logic' back together again. I don't think anybody found this particularly satisfactory — the resultant dramatic structure providing a basic pattern of rationality spotted with isolated and inchoate irruptions of 'the irrational'.

This gave me the idea of reversing the procedure: instead of working through the scene and elucidating it with an a priori set of 'rational' assumptions, what would happen if one started with the 'irrational' moment? If, instead of treating it as a wholly inscrutable aberration, one posited it as the key to everything else? What if — as Heidegger might have put it — one chose to 'dwell' in the irrational moment, making that one's theoretical ground? How does one theorise the irrational? It was this chain of thought that led me to seduction. Clearly, it would be quixotic to hope to discover a coherent 'logic' in seduction but it might nevertheless exhibit characteristic processes which could be described or even adumbrated. In Chapter Two, I advance certain theoretical postulates relevant to seduction — for which I am particularly indebted to the writings of Jean Baudrillard. I would also like to acknowledge the assistance of Danny Boyle and the RSC company of *The Bite of the Night*, Kenny Ireland and the Wrestling School company of *Victory*, David Thomas, David Ian Rabey and Roland Cotterill for reading and commenting on my work. Particular thanks are due to Howard Barker for being most generous with advice and assistance.

INTRODUCTION

In spite of being widely recognised as 'a major voice', Barker's relationship with British theatre has not blossomed as one might have expected. In the seventies, his career developed initially along lines similar to a number of other 'political' dramatists such as Brenton, Hare and Churchill. Having achieved a degree of success and recognition at The Royal Court with *Stripwell* (1975) and *Fair Slaughter* (1977), his work was taken up by The RSC Warehouse Company which staged *That Good Between Us* (1977), *The Hang of The Gaol* (1978), and *The Loud Boy's Life* (1980). These plays were received as part of the Warehouse's programme of politically committed work. Howard Davies, the artistic director of the Warehouse, said of *That Good Between Us*:

> *I was keen to do a play by one of the writers who were linguistically orientated and belonged to the tradition of, if you like, intellectual socialists — Howard Brenton, David Edgar, Howard Barker.*[1]

The overt and consciously political slant of this company tended to obscure for many critics other less immediately categorisable facets of Barker's plays. So, Ronald Hayman could write of *The Hang of the Gaol*:

> *What is ultimately stultifying for the audience is the inescapable feeling that each confrontation is being rigged to serve as an illustration for a thesis about class-war, that the dialogue is being written not to penetrate more searchingly into the theatrical reality which the fiction is generating, but to vent a spleen that existed in toto before Howard Barker began to concern himself with these characters or this situation. His interest in people and behaviour is secondary.*[2]

Slightly more perceptive leftist critics, however, voiced the suspicion that Barker's work was not essentially informed by conscious political commitment. W. Stephen Gilbert, in a review of *Fair Slaughter*, compared the play unfavourably with the Brechtian style of Bond:

> *The trick in Bond's plays is that the analysis percolates the theatricality, that the latter is a precise manifestation of the former. FAIR SLAUGHTER is not as clear and eloquent. It's a nicely judged pageant history of British Communism, but I'm not sure that Barker's unprecedented engagement with his characters doesn't finally fudge his conclusion —*[3]

At the same time, there was a growing complaint about the lack of authenticity and realism (see Hayman above) which led James Fenton to dismiss *The Loud Boy's Life* in contemptuous terms:

> *The play… knows nothing of Britain and nothing of politics. It doesn't want to know. It merely caters sycophantically to the prejudices of a pseudo-political milieu.*[4]

This kind of blinkered and at times violent critical response to the plays, reflecting more the political or ideological prejudices of the reviewer, did little to assist a balanced assessment of their more unique and artistically radical qualities. As I have already indicated, Barker's work in the seventies generally recommended itself to directors on a 'political' level: this was because the plays were overtly concerned with political figures and political questions. Besides, it was clear that Barker's sympathies lay on the left. The political overview, however, served for some time to mask a shift in Barker's interest away from the political to the personal, from the stereotype to the individual. The vogue for political theatre had, however, facilitated a general formal and stylistic diversification — with satiric caricature being particularly favoured. Indeed, Barker himself admits that, for a time early in his career, he allowed the satiric impulse to dominate — as in *Edward, The Final Days* (1972):

> *I placed the characters in EDWARD, THE FINAL DAYS squarely in their social context, but only as subjects of lampoon, because I hated them and was offended by them. I am still deeply offended by society, and still hate as much, but the habit is no longer iconoclastic, as it was automatically then…. In that period I was further from any feeling of involvement with my characters than at any time before or since. I began to feel that being involved with my characters at all was a weakness.*[5]

Claw (1975), however, marked the end of this tendency and constitutes a landmark in Barker's artistic development. The action begins in familiar 'knockabout' style tracing the career of an ambitious working class youth from a background of deprivation. Noel Biledew is born, the illegitimate son of Mrs Biledew, a munitions worker, while her husband languishes in a German POW camp. When Biledew returns home his anger at this unanticipated 'son' is compounded by the fact that he has meanwhile been rendered sexually impotent through a violent encounter with the boot of a camp guard. Biledew, a brooding idealist, is presented as inflexibly and intensely 'moral' in the cause of communism. Mrs Biledew, on the contrary, is thoroughly pragmatic and prepared to brush aside moral scruples when these might conflict with her own material comfort or social advancement. Accordingly, when the infant Noel returns home from school with thirty coronation mugs which have been traded for 'a look' at Joan Preston 'behind the lavatories', maternal disgust rapidly gives way to approbation and his enterprise is compared favourably to his unemployed father's torpor. To an extent, Noel's subsequent career can be seen as his attempt to reconcile the conflicting imperatives of this genealogy — on the one hand Biledew's moralised class loyalty/class hatred and Mrs Biledew's amoral selfish pragmatism.

Apart from this, Noel's poor eyesight has made him an object of hatred and derision:

> NOEL: *I'm used to being hated. From the first day I went to the Infants school they had it in for me. Because of these. (He touches his glasses).*[6]

> NOEL: *Serve who? The sods who hid my glasses so I wandered round the playground with my hands outstretched, calling out 'Boss eyes' and 'Blind git' and making me fall on my face?*[7]

Noel's personal response to a cruel world is hatred and a desire for vengeance. Although he is the central character in the play, he is not thereby accorded any privileged moral status.

He follows up his coronation mug success by embarking on a career as a pimp with his first employee being a fellow comrade in the Young Communist League. The way he secures Nora's services is typical of a series of crucial moments in which Noel recreates himself in his new, self-styled identity of 'Claw'. He persuades her — appealing to her desire for a better life while simultaneously neutralising the moral taboo by presenting prostitution as a form of class war:

> NOEL: *This is political action! (She stops, her back to him) This isn't theory. This isn't arguing the toss for the millioneth time in the Battersea cell of the world revolutionary party. This is action, this is carrying anthrax into their woolly nests.*
> *(Pause. She turns, looks at him for some seconds.)*
> NORA: *And what's my share?*
> NOEL: *Halves.*
> NORA: *No.*
> *(Pause)*
> NOEL: *All right. 60–40.*
> *(She grins)*
> NORA: *Rip their soiled knickers down!*
> NOEL: *Hero of Labour!*
> NORA: *How do we start?*
> NOEL: *Right here. Tonight. Start small and local, then spread our wings.*
> NORA: *There aren't any bourgeois in this street.*
> NOEL: *Of course not. This is just for the experience.*
> *(She takes a deep breath)*

NORA: All right.
NOEL: First geezer comes along, I proposition him.[8]

What happens here is typical of a process which, I will argue later, lies at the heart of Barker's dramatic method. Noel's proposal, contravening as it does the moral taboo, provokes, initially, simple outrage. Persuasion, however, arouses curiosity and the proposal becomes a challenge. When Nora takes up Noel's suggestion, both are exhilarated through accepting the notion of transgression and proceed to escalate theory into action. In the event, Noel has to face the challenge of importuning a policeman (the 'first geezer') and though in strictly material terms he comes out a net loser, he is both rich in experience and launched in his career. It becomes clear, however, as the play progresses that Noel's success in selling Nora the idea of prostitution as class war was no mere cynical casuistry deployed solely for immediate material gain: in convincing Nora, he has, simultaneously, convinced himself. He rejects his communist father's posture of a fruitless but 'moral' political defiance and attempts to achieve the private satisfaction of undermining the hated establishment from within; eventually he rises to the dizzy heights of supplying prostitutes to the Home Secretary. This provides the ideal opportunity in Act Two for the bulk of the play's savagely humorous political satire.

Noel's crusade is complicated, however, when he falls in love with his distinguished client's wife, a turn of events which leads him into confrontation. The moment he is perceived as a real threat to the political establishment, he is detained in a mental hospital and liquidated; his murder comprises the third act of the play. Of this scene, Barker has said:

> *I knew when I'd written CLAW... that I'd made a definite advance, largely because of the third act, which I regarded as a triumph. It was almost a new form for me: in prose with very long speeches — even longer to begin with than they are in the final text.*
> *There was a withdrawal from the action on my part, too: it is less insistent. Nothing in the act relies on the shared assumptions that I have expected audiences to respond to in other acts. It was the beginning of a confidence to remove myself from a common ground. I dislike a play in which the dramatist overstates his intentions, making matters easy for his audience. It produces this rather unhealthy expectation that we should all know what it's about by the interval. To continually undermine the expected is the only way to alter people's perceptions.*[9]

Act 2 ends confrontationally with Noel wrestling psychologically and physically with Clapcott, the Home Secretary, as a special branch officer armed with a machine gun bursts in through the window. Act 3 is set in 'an institution' where breakfast is about to be served to a single diner. Lily and Lusby, attired as waiters with white jackets and napkins, address the audience in turn with lengthy monologues of reminiscence which gradually reveal that one is an ex-terrorist, the other a redundant hangman. Both men are phlegmatically psychopathic and the leisurely and reflective pace of these speeches serves transitionally to wean the audience from expectations of hectic comic action towards a change of style.

Noel enters in 'a battered grey suit' and they serve him breakfast. Apart from its sacramental implications, the eating of food upon stage can be a very significant theatrical action – here fruit juice, bacon, eggs, and tea; this consumption is physical — and, in itself, real. By extension it serves to emphasise the reality of the character and — further — the situation, acting as a device to alter our focus on Noel rapidly and economically; cartoon characters aren't substantial in this way. There is no 'human' contact between the waiters and their client. As Noel eats, the reflective monologues carry on, with occasional lengthy pauses, specified by Barker as lasting up to ten seconds; these serve to increase the tension already created by the lack of on-stage communication.

When Noel first speaks he is 'tense and desperate', — a startling contrast to his two gaolers, and his speech is a plea for help, an expression of his feelings of impotence and terror; here Barker makes use of a device which he frequently employs to create a powerful emotional effect swiftly — the cry:

> (*Long pause. Then with a cry of despair*) My home! My ordinary nothingness! I would fall
> down on the grass and kiss it no matter how many dogs had shit on it....[10]

After another pause, Lusby resumes his monologue and the audience are finally given to understand how both men were recruited to form 'a handpicked team to deal with a special category of criminals.' Their impassivity and casual conversation about the sexual proclivities of various pop singers contrast with Claw's desperate desire to live. In this extremity he summons up the hitherto despised figure of his father now dying in the geriatric ward of a hospital 'in the stench of urine and terminal flesh'. After a moving colloquy in which father and son show tenderness for the only time, Old Biledew advises Noel to —

> Win them with your common suffering. Find the eloquence of Lenin, lick their cruelty away…
> Don't despise them, win them Noel!… Be cogent, earn their love —[11]

then leaves him alone with his gaolers. After a pause, the son follows this advice in a speech of some sixty lines, an appeal to their humanity and sense of class loyalty which accumulates an enormous emotional charge. Barker's stage directions read:

(This speech must begin clumsily and brokenly. By the end it is eloquent and delivered with conviction. It is the significant transformation of the play.)[12]

For the audience, who know Lily and Lusby, Noel's task appears hopeless but the quality of this speech is such that by the end there should be real suspense as to its effect. Noel transforms himself and has possibly transformed his situation. After a long expressionless pause, their decision is signalled by Lily's switching on his transistor radio which is playing 'Hungry for Love' and a bath is lowered in. The horror of the execution is emphasised in the details of the stage directions:

(Lily and Lusby rise to their feet and roll up their sleeves. After some time, Noel begins slowly to undress, removing first his jacket, then his shirt, then trousers, shoes, socks, and finally pants, he goes slowly to the bath and climbs in. With a single thrust, Lily and Lusby force his head beneath the water.)[13]

The theatrical impact of Noel's stripping, apart from its symbolic aptness, serves to reinforce the tragic intensity of this moment; we are a million miles from the cartoon style of Act One, yet Barker has managed successfully to link these two apparently incompatible extremes and forge an artistic whole with a unique integrity of its own. Such was the 'definite advance' which he felt he had made in this scene:

When I wrote CLAW, I was vaguely aware that I was getting on a helter-skelter of satire and I wasn't being at all engaged with my characters. It was only with CLAW that I managed to drag myself back from what might have been a fatal precipice. The last act which I still think is rather a fine piece of writing surmounts and overcomes the satirical emphasis of the previous two acts. So I was led off and recovered. (Laughs)[14]

Retrospectively it is possible to see how the satirical impulse leading to the development of a style employing rhetoric, exaggeration and the grotesque ultimately helped Barker to forge his own non-realistic style of fantasy in which the satirical element has now all but disappeared. More recently he has stated:

The time for satire is ended. Nothing can be satirised in the authoritarian state. It is culture reduced to playing the spoons. The stockbroker laughs and the satirist plays the spoons.[15]

The sense of caricature has been increasingly marginal, has been located in minor characters. In the centre of the plays complexity and contradiction have replaced it. Partly this reflects moves away from class stereotypes.[16]

The incident of Noel Biledew attempting persuasion in an apparently hopeless situation both exemplifies and symbolises a shift in Barker's interest; it manifests several preoccupations to which he was to return repeatedly in later plays. Firstly, there is the catastrophic scenario:

> *Under ordinary circumstances character remains unexplored, — unexposed; the nerves are quite concealed. But in order to force that exposure on the characters, I always set them within catastrophic situations. The characters on stage are not simply in unlikely situations but usually disastrous ones... I'm attracted to those circumstances because at times like that people are disorderly. They cease to be the predictable product of social forces — not simply workers or bourgeois or rentiers; they are dislocated from those classic roles by the social struggle.*[17]

Secondly, there is the individual attempt to produce an alteration in the apparently inevitable — solely through speech; Noel's effort is mirrored in the climactic confrontation of *Stripwell* (Royal Court 1975): in *Claw* a working-class rebel pleads with establishment assassins; Stripwell, high court judge and pillar of the establishment, begs for his life at the hands of an anarchic criminal who is about to shoot him. In *Fair Slaughter* (Royal Court 1977), the plot of the play turns upon the prisoner, Old Gocher, succeeding in persuading the gaoler, Leary, to help him escape. In *Crimes In Hot Countries* (1983), the magician and rabble-rouser, Toplis, recounts how he persuaded guards to let him escape from custody the night before he was due to be executed for desertion: two successful permutations of Claw's dilemma. In *The Power of the Dog*, Ilona tries desperately to persuade Stalin to spare her lover, the corrupt Sorge. There are numerous similar instances of attempts at persuasive speech in extremis. At a more profound level, Barker seems fascinated by the power of language to effect the social event and the individual. This exploratory impulse tends to supersede the simple polemic consistent with satire, and *Stripwell*, premiered in the same year as *Claw*, left some critics who had found the latter play 'legible' as political satire, confused as to where Barker's sympathies lay.[18]

Just as the predominantly conventional forms, even though disrupted, in *Claw* and *Stripwell*, maintained the accessibility of the plays — in the eyes of theatre managements at least — so the political/satirical elements of the Warehouse plays and Barker's very considerable comic gifts ensured their appeal to a contemporary appetite for political drama. It was becoming increasingly evident, however, that his writing was growing in complexity with far fewer concessions being made to conventional expectations. The RSC's commitment to staging Barker (albeit this commitment had extended only as far as studio spaces) faltered when they rejected *Crimes In Hot Countries* — a script which they themselves had commissioned. At that time, this was, arguably, the most densely written Barker text to date. The drama was not really satire, nor clear political allegory — and it certainly wasn't realism.

The eighties evidenced a growing rejection of Barker's work by the major theatrical instutions. The National Theatre had never shown any real interest. The RSC staged a 'season' of Barker plays in the Pit but the productions were notoriously meagre while the company channelled all its institutional energies and resources into launching *Les Miserables*. *The Bite of the Night* was staged in similar circumstances. *The Europeans*, written for the RSC, was rejected by them. There have been productions of Barker plays at The Royal Court but these have frequently been promoted as collaborations by actor-led companies such as Joint Stock and, latterly, The Wrestling School. *The Bite of the Night* was originally submitted to the Court and eventually rejected by them. Outside London, Barker has had occasional commissions from more adventurous regional theatres such as Sheffield Crucible (*The Love of a Good Man* (1978) and *A Passion in Six Days* (1983)).

As Robert Shaughnessy indicates in an essay which purports to analyse 'the Barker phenomenon'[19], Barker's main supporters within theatre have been actors, — a state of affairs which culminated in the formation of a company devoted exclusively to performing Barker's work — The Wrestling School. This grew out of earlier Joint Stock productions (*Victory* (1983) and *The Power of the Dog* (1984)) and it is interesting that this particular company, dedicated to democratic self-organisation should have abandoned its characteristic process of company-evolved drama in favour of a text-based approach. In the essay cited above, Shaughnessy develops his argument by claiming that the actor Ian McDiarmid is 'a sort of spokesman for the author' and by drawing upon McDiarmid's conceptions of the essential qualities of the plays. His conclusion is:

> *Actors, then, enjoy performing Barker's work because it presents them with the opportunity consciously and ostentatiously to display their skills as performers.*[20]

Shaughnessy, although he admits later that Barker's dialogue does contain 'a radical disruptive potential', continues this theme by suggesting that Barker's poetic 'style' is essentially an attempt to promote Barker in the role of the 'unique authorial figure', a project in which he is abetted by actors who wish to 'show off'. This somewhat threadbare formulation does not really address what one might perhaps be forgiven for regarding as the key issue — the quality of the actual plays. Regarding this, however, Shaughnessy's analysis of 'the Barker phenomenon' extends only to a single speech from the first page of *The Castle*.

The fact that it has been left to actors to champion Barker is no accident but reflects the inadequacy of current theoretical orthodoxies relating to the production of plays. The key figure in this respect is the director, who carries final responsibility for transferring text to stage and establishes the philosophical/theoretical approach of the company. Actors tend through the nature of their work to function more instinctively. The emergence of the director as a pivotal figure has been well documented in modern theatre studies and this canon (Brecht, Stanislavsky, Meyerhold, Artaud, Grotowski, Brook etc.) has become a significant element in the educational mythology of the contemporary director. A concomitant movement has been the downgrading of dramatist and text. In the words of Jean Mounet-Sully — 'Chaque texte n'est qu'un prétexte'. The extreme instance of this tendency towards creative control by director is to be found in the case of the film auteur who will instruct a writer to produce text for predetermined scenarios. In the theatre, a corresponding authority has, to an extent, been exercised by directors, who have had a considerable role in shaping the final performance text of new plays. While it is now the norm for theatrical practice to make demands upon text, there seems to be little expectation that text should make demands upon practice — other than in the case of purely technical ('special') effects. Barker's texts, moreover, are not only very demanding intellectually, but run completely counter to most of the orthodoxies of received directorial wisdom.

For a considerable period during the seventies and eighties, progressive theatre in Britain was dominated by the influence of Brecht. Though this has begun to wane somewhat with the collapse of the Eastern European régimes, it remains a powerful element in that nothing has appeared to challenge or indeed replace it. While it is true that there were other countervailing forces such as Artaud and indeed a huge range of theatrical experiment, no particular element of this sustained and developed itself as consistently and pervasively as the Brechtian thematic. There are many reasons for this but by no means the least significant must be that Brecht's theatrical ideals were closely linked to the wider social project of the Marxism he espoused. He left not only a significant corpus of plays and records of his own theatrical practice but also a body of theoretical work which sets a framework of technique and a relatively coherent programme dedicated to a new ideal — the Theatre for a Scientific Age. As stated, his influence on all aspects of the British theatre has been widespread but nowhere is this more evident than in the cases of the director, William Gaskill, and the dramatist, Edward Bond.

As Artistic Director of the Royal Court Theatre for many years, Gaskill occupied a key position regarding the British stage in that this company were pre-eminent — certainly from the mid-fifties to the seventies — in developing new dramatic writing and innovative approaches to performance. Gaskill built on to the realist, socially concerned, 'kitchen sink' style of the early Osborne/Arden/Wesker plays a growing awareness of Brechtian stagecraft and theatrical praxis which informed decisively the dramaturgy of Edward Bond and a whole generation of 'Court-trained' directors. In fact, he established a house-style at the Court which still prevailed into the nineties under the aegis of one of his successors as Artistic Director, Max Stafford-Clark. The actor's focus of attention was directed away from the individual psychology of the character and towards the socio-economic significance of their behaviour. This process is well exemplified in the 'lesson' of the cadged cigarette with which Gaskill commenced rehearsals of *Mother Courage* with the Royal Shakespeare Company (1962).

> *I decided to begin with a simple Socratic dialogue. I cadged a cigarette from one of the actresses... and then asked the group why she had given me the cigarette. The first answers were all psychological — her generosity, her sycophancy, my meanness. Very gradually I led them to understand that the action was a social action and a habitual one, in which the economic value of the cigarette was a factor. This led to very simple improvisations which were always followed by an analysis of the actions in the scene. In a two-handed scene each actor would narrate the actions as objectively as possible, sometimes in the third person, and this narration was analysed over and over again till both actors would agree on the exact sequence of events; that is, they would tell the same story.*[21]

Clearly, the cigarette here is part of a pattern of interpersonal relations but Gaskill insists on elevating the object to a dominant role and furthermore the identity of the object is no longer dependent upon the particular interpersonal context; it has become a 'thing-in-itself' because it has 'economic value' — a reference to an external value structure. This approach is carried through into staging with the tendency to foreground solid, selected objects as properties. The characters then have the possibility of relating not only to each other, but directly to objects which have ceased to be merely instrumental. Bond, who absorbed much of Gaskill's 'Brechtian' theory, exemplifies this dramatic interest in the object. Even in a play as early as *Saved* (1965), for instance, not only is the cigarette, like the copy of the Radio Times, an issue in interpersonal relations but the pram and the chair, in terms of their economic significance, their weight and behavioural characteristics, play important roles in the development of the action.

Gaskill's dramaturgy, of which the cigarette 'dialogue' provides a paradigm, reflects an analysis of human interaction based on exchange value, an extension and analogue of the operations of capitalist society. As a system it is logical, coherent and clear. This latter quality, clarity, was one of the hallmarks of Gaskill's direction which is, again, thoroughly Brechtian. The insistence that the actors should arrive at 'the same story' removes the possibility of ambiguity and ensures that in conflict situations the audience will nevertheless be presented with a single view. For a didactic theatre, this is a logical process. It amounts to interpreting the actions presented. As used to be said of Brecht — we are presented not with 'life' but 'an analysis of life'. Brecht himself was particularly concerned that audiences should come away from his plays with the correct message; to this end, in his work with the Berliner Ensemble he was continually fine tuning performances in order to manipulate audience sympathies more effectively — *Mother Courage* and *The Life of Galileo* being notable examples.

Whereas at one time it was widely considered that Brecht and Stanislavsky represented opposite polarities with regard to theatrical production, this view has since been challenged and it has become clear that both practically and theoretically the two have much in common.[22] Both focus upon a concept of reality: Stanislavsky, as the supreme engineer of stage realism, making 'truth' the holy grail of acting; Brecht being so reality-conscious that he insists on theatre alerting the audience continually to its status as a mere second-order phenomenon — a representation. Both insist upon the supreme importance of what Stanislavsky referred to as the 'Ruling Idea', — that is a predetermined principle, thematic or 'message' which would subsequently act as a selective criterion to which every aspect of the mise en scène must be subordinated. Both approaches were rigorously analytic and rationalistic, Stanislavsky insisting that his actors should devise personal throughlines, unbroken chains of objectives which had to be both logical and coherent. For every moment they were on stage the actor had to have formulated a motivation for their character. These were to be expressed in the form of 'I want to…' followed by a verb. When performing, the actor could engage with their character's psychology through identifying with the objective and projecting in the imagination its fulfillment. Needless to say this makes a number of presumptions about human behaviour, — that it is always logical and always clearly motivated with these motivations being unmixed and conscious. In practice this technique works best when characters are being 'single-minded' or businesslike. It does not sum up the whole range of human behaviour. What it does do, however, is facilitate the clear presentation of radically simplified interpretations of this. Which is why the formulation of objectives became integral to the Brechtianism of Gaskill and his successors.

The general ubiquity today of Stanislavsky-based teaching in drama schools reflects the extent of the widespread influence of this reductive rationalism in the theatre. The original aims of the Moscow Art Theatre were identical to those of the Enlightenment: according to Stanislavsky —

> *We are trying to create the first rational, moral public theatre and it is to this lofty aim we dedicate our lives.*[23]

In this respect, Stanislavsky's attitude was consonant with the traditional progressive ideals of the Russian intelligentsia of his day. Jean Benedetti argues further the particular influence of Tolstoy:

> *Tolstoy is the final great influence on Stanislavski's views on aesthetics. In 1898, he published his essay, 'What Is Art?' in which he advanced the notion that a work of art must be immediately intelligible and of moral use to simple, unsophisticated minds, without the need for commentary or explanation. It must be 'transparent'… the idea of 'transparent action' became central to Stanislavski's thinking…*[24]

The 'transparent' dramatic action is an action which exposes its 'truth' and 'truth' equals 'the rational' equals 'the moral'. Regarding this, one of the most useful aspects of the Stanislavsky System is the emphasis laid on the quality of Naivety and on the actor cultivating a 'natural' stage presence, the naive persona being essentially 'transparent'.

In 'A Short Organum for the Theatre' (1948), Brecht clearly accepts the Marxist elevation of Science as the touchstone of ultimate truth:

> *The bourgeois class, which owes to science an advancement that it was able, by ensuring that it alone enjoyed the fruits, to convert into domination, knows very well that its rule would come to an end if the scientific eye were turned on its own undertakings.*[25]

For Brecht, this provided the progressive theatre with its proper mission, which was to sweep away the mystificatory and reactionary culture of the bourgeoisie and to encourage a scientific consideration of social relations and human behaviour. Although his 'representations' should never directly create the illusion of reality thereby risking mere escapist trance, the real world, as opposed to the illusory fantasies of 'false consciousness', is nevertheless very much what Brechtion theatre is all about:

> *The theatre has to become geared into reality if it is to be in a position to turn out effective representations of reality, and to be allowed to do so.*
> *24. But this makes it simpler for the theatre to edge as close as possible to the apparatus of education and mass communication. For although we cannot bother it with the raw material of knowledge in all its variety, which would stop it from being enjoyable, it is still free to find enjoyment in teaching and enquiring. It constructs its workable representations of society, which are then in a position to influence society, wholly and entirely as a game: for those who are constructing society it sets out society's experiences, past and present alike, in such a manner that the audience can 'appreciate' the feelings, insights and impulses which are distilled by the wisest, most active and most passionate among us from the events of the day or the century.*[26]

I have quoted this passage in full because it seems to me to illustrate a number of significant points about Brechtian theatre: firstly the importance of the 'reality' principle is clearly indicated and the mechanistic ('geared into'/'workable') and economistic ('turned out'/'apparatus'/'raw material'/'distilled') metaphors emphasise the nature of this reality. Secondly, there is a clear endorsement of an academicism (in the pejorative sense of this word): audiences are not to be troubled with the 'raw material' of knowledge since they are not capable of 'appreciating' this. Instead they are to be the recipients of the suitably processed ('distilled') 'feelings, insights and impulses' of an elite ('the most passionate etc.') Thirdly, the hitherto implicit authoritarianism is rendered explicit: theatre must conform to this prescription — 'to be allowed'. Here, Brecht's comment concerning 'the apparatus of education and mass communication' is interestingly prophetic of the increasing subordination of 'educational' processes to closed structures of objectives, ruling ideas and of 'experiments' which, while offering the semblance of open enquiry, are rigged to produce the 'correct' knowledge.

Edward Bond, above all other British dramatists, demonstrates in both his plays and copious theoretical writings, a most profound Brechtian influence. With Bond, the Science ideal becomes Reason or Rationality which is, in turn, equated with reality:

> *There's a specialism in art just as there is in technology and politics. It only becomes embarrassing when the artist suggests he's a specialist in another, finer world. He's a specialist in describing this world, and all art is realism. We're the product of material circumstances and there's no place in art for mysticism or obscurantism. Art is the illustration, illumination, expression of rationality — not something primitive, dark, the primal urge or anything like that.*[27]

After his initial *succès de scandale* with *Saved*, Bond went on with *The Narrow Road to the Deep North* (1968) to forge a literary/poetic style leading to a series of plays — *Lear* (1971), *The Sea* (1973), *Bingo* (1973), *The Fool* (1975) — which met with a degree of critical success that established his status as a contemporary classic. It was also significant that those involved in producing these plays, especially the directors, understood clearly the Royal Court/Brechtian principles of their stagecraft.

The approach to performance of the Court, their 'house style', has been widely influential beyond the confines of Sloane Square. Not only has this theatre been a significant 'training ground' for young directors but it has been a force to be reckoned by all those concerned with 'progressive' theatre. Howard Davies, discussing the beginnings of a career which has since brought him to the National Theatre, describes how, as director of the

New Vic Studio in Bristol in the early '70s, he sought to engage Royal Court actors:

> *The only way I could implement the new play policy I was hoping to initiate was to rely upon actors who'd worked with Gaskill or Stafford-Clark and who understood the language of those plays, those writers and those fringe groups with whom they'd been associated.*[28]

Davies went on to the RSC where he firmly established his Brechtian credentials by directing Brecht's *Man Is Man, Schweik in the Second World War*, Bond's *Bingo* and *The Bundle*. He was in overall control of the RSC Warehouse in London which during its brief existence staged a remarkable series of new plays. Of the three by Barker, one, *The Loud Boy's Life*, was directed by Davies. *The Hang of The Gaol* was directed by an associate, Bill Alexander, who had worked with Davies at The New Vic Studio in Bristol — 'we talk the same language'[29] — and had come to the Warehouse via The Royal Court and RSC Stratford. He subsequently went on to direct two more Barker plays in The Pit at the Barbican — *Crimes in Hot Countries* and *Downchild*. At the Royal Court itself eight Barker plays have been staged — two directed by Gaskill — *Cheek* (1970) and *Women Beware Women* (1986), — also *No One Was Saved* (1970), *Stripwell* (1975). *Fair Slaughter* (1977), *No End of Blame* (1981), *Victory* (1983) and *The Last Supper* (1988). Danny Boyle, who directed *Victory* and later *The Bite of the Night* at the RSC Pit (1988), described himself as 'Court-trained' with a Brechtian/Marxist approach to production.[30] Unfortunately, Barker's dramatic texts do not match up to the very clear notions which directors such as Gaskill, Stafford-Clark, Davies and Alexander have of what a play should be and the Gaskill/Stafford-Clark directorial tradition, strongly rooted in Brecht, Stanislavsky and social realism, finds itself at a loss when it attempts to 'analyse' a Barker text.

I have used the example of the third act of *Claw* to suggest how even at this early stage in his artistic development, Barker was headed in an altogether different direction from the prevailing realist/Brechtian ideal: rather than demonstrate character conforming to social type, he was drawn to exploring character dislocated from the social by means of the catastrophic. Because the social is increasingly being experienced as all reality, such dislocations are often described as 'unreal'. Evidence for this is available in the cases of the small number of people in our society who do experience catastrophe — war, major accidents etc. — and consequently have great difficulty in re-integrating themselves back into 'social reality'. In taking this course, Barker was, as he states, removing his work from the common ground of shared assumptions and reverting in a very radical sense to the characteristic ambiguities and sheer suspense of drama. It will be recalled that the Brechtian epic method tends to negate the suspense element by presenting the action in historicised form so that audiences may focus on the 'how' rather than the 'what'. Such was the blanket degree of critical incomprehension — as exampled by the reviews quoted at the beginning of this chapter — that Barker eventually felt compelled to defend and create a space for his own work. This began with an article entitled 'Fortynine Asides for a Tragic Theatre' which was printed in *The Guardian* in 1986 and eventually lead to the publication of *Arguments for a Theatre* in 1989 which collected all his critical writings to date. Fortunately, the previous year saw the first production by the actor-led Wrestling School, which took up the challenge the theatrical establishment was intent on sloughing off. Since the late eighties, the Wrestling School has been at the forefront of staging new Barker plays with *The Last Supper* (1988), *Seven Lears* (1989), *The Europeans* (1993), and *Hated Nightfall* (1994), — the latter directed by Barker himself. If one compares the following extract from Barker's 'Arguments' with the quotations from Brecht and Bond cited above, then the full extent of his apostasy becomes apparent:

> *The Theatre of Catastrophe addresses itself to those who suffer the maiming of the imagination. All mechanical art, all ideological art, (the entertaining, the informative) intensifies the pain but simultaneously heightens the unarticulated desire for the restitution of moral speculation, which is the business of theatre. The Theatre of Catastrophe is therefore a theatre for the offended. It has no dialogue with*
> > *Those who make poles of narrative and character*
> > *Those who proclaim clarity and responsibility*[31]

> *The real end of drama in this period must be not the reproduction of reality, critical or otherwise, (the traditional model of the Royal Court play, socialistic, voyeuristic) but speculation — not what is (now unbearably decadent) but what might be, what is imaginable. The subject then becomes not man-in-society, but knowledge itself, and the protagonist not the man of action (rebel or capitalist as source of pure energy) but the struggler with self. So in an era when sexuality is simultaneously cheap, domestic and soon-to-be-forbidden, desire becomes the field of enquiry most likely to stimulate a creative disorder.*[32]

Perhaps the central irony of the whole 'rational' rhetoric focusses on Brecht's contention — also propounded by Bond — that the field of culture lags behind the development of the physical sciences, that the new scientific thinking has not been brought to bear on human relations and that this, above all, should be the project of a genuinely progressive theatre. In fact, both Brecht's and Bond's supposedly 'scientific' thinking belongs essentially to the nineteenth century, their 'reason' being grounded in a Newtonian universe of absolute space and absolute time regulated by absolute mechanical 'laws' of cause and effect. 'Rational Theatre' is a stranger not only to contemporary Chaos Theory but also to Quantum Theory and even to Einstein's Theory of Relativity evolved almost a century ago. It is to the intellectual upheavals concomitant with and consequent upon such scientific revolutions and how these reflect on the demand for reality in drama — Brechtian or Stanislavskian — that I wish to turn in the next chapter.

1

POSTMODERNISM AND THEATRE

Bond has stated that:

History is the struggle for reason.[1]

and it has frequently and with some justification been claimed that reason comprises the foundations of the technologically advanced world we live in today. Likewise it is commonplace to trace the origins of this technological progress and the formation of the great intellectual 'disciplines' which have informed it back to the seventeenth and eighteenth centuries, 'the Age of Reason' and 'the Enlightenment'. As one first encounters them today, the discourses of the physical and social sciences such as Biology, Physics, Economics, Psychology or Linguistics, manifest themselves as repositories of abstract, truth-based structures which underlie and *in-form* the world of superficial appearances. They fall from the sky upon the young mind with a perfection and absence of origin just like the new Citroën in Barthes' eponymous essay.[2] If the internal coherence and rationality of these discourses were insufficient of itself to extinguish incredulity, one is confronted everywhere with the overwhelming evidence of their works; in a similar way the ubiquity of Christian institutions in Medieval times must have served to confirm the faith in all but the most sophisticated of sceptics.

Each of these discourses has defined its field, set up its boundaries and established procedures and validation processes for determining its truths and for those authorised to disseminate them. Interlocking with the discourses are political and social power networks. Furthermore, the discourses themselves are concerned directly with power, in that (and here the physical sciences tend to serve as a paradigm for the others) they aim to provide the possesser of knowledge with the capacity to manipulate and control — this being perhaps the ultimate touchstone of validity for 'scientific truth'.

In the introductory essay to his classic text, *The Age of Enlightenment*, Isaiah Berlin characterises the social project of the eighteenth century rationalists thus:

> *... they also believed, if anything even more strongly than their empiricist adversaries, that the truth was one single, harmonious body of knowledge... that all the sciences and all the faiths, the most fanatical superstitions and the most savage customs, when 'cleansed' of their irrational elements by the advance of civilisation, can be harmonised in the final true philosophy which could solve all theoretical and practical problems for all men everywhere for all time.[3]*

In practice, however, the project is not unproblematical: one person's reason can be another's irrationality. In particular, it is reason's urge to validate what it has already instituted as rational that should inspire a level of caution. Hegel was aware of this in his description of 'rational' ontology:

> *Reason is the certainty of consciousness that it is all reality...*

> *It demonstrates itself to be this along the path in which first, in the dialectic movement of 'meaning', perceiving and understanding, **otherness as an intrinsic being vanishes**.[4] (my emphasis)*

Edward Bond puts it more bluntly:

> *Our species can no longer live with the irrational.[5]*

> *The struggle for rationalism is of course against irrationalism. That's why it may have to be violent.[6]*

Not surprisingly, one of the first tasks the devotees of Reason set themselves was the defining, confining and 'curing' of the irrational human mind — madness.

If what is referred to as postmodernist thought may be said to share any general features in common, perhaps the most obvious of these is a resistence to this totalising and totalitarian tendency of reason. In the second half of this century, a massive work of discursive deconstruction has seriously questioned the integrity and the truth-based authority of all the 'rational' disciplines. This critique has been levelled at their theoretical bases with critical distances being established through methods such as *traduction* (critical concepts from one discipline are deployed against another, e.g. linguistic concepts in psychology — Lacan) or, most spectacularly, through assisted autocatalysis where a critical concept is deployed against itself (Derrida) — or for that matter a whole discipline — the history of history, the repressions of psychology etc. (Baudrillard). Foucault, in particular, demonstrated the possibilities of what might otherwise be dismissed as mere 'theory' by writing alternative discourses such as *Madness and Civilisation — A History of Insanity in the Age of Reason* as well as all his famous 'archaeologies' of the human sciences. It is as if the whole apparatus of the truth-producing machine had been turned against itself. To reveal? — the elliptical, the aleatory, the arbitrary, political expediency, ultimate evasions which constitute a betrayal of their proper dialectic. In almost all cases, an original act of violence, a founding repression.

Culturally speaking, the shock waves of deconstruction are potentially as devastating as those of the theory of relativity. It takes some effort to realise the extent to which our 'world' is not merely grounded in, but fabricated by these authoritative discourses. What is 'the human' when we discard Biology, Psychology, Sociology and History? — originally grids for analysing the human but latterly models for fabricating the same, our understanding of ourselves and each other is permeated with assumptions derived from these disciplines. Furthermore our conception of the human is fleshed out and continually reinforced in the 'realistic' fictions of the mass media. Whether these are satisfying voyeuristic or escapist impulses, providing vicarious sadistic gratification or the reassurance of the known, the mode of representation seeks almost invariably — within the constraints imposed by its function, its 'formula' — to achieve authenticity — i.e. recognition. Television, in particular, exhibits two convergent processes — the authentication of the fictional and the fictionalising of the authentic. In the latter, the real — such as 'fly-on-the-wall' style documentary or a sporting event — is processed according to rules of dramatic presentation — exposition, build-up of suspense around a central event, resolution etc. Not only do such fictions 'explicate' human behaviour but they almost invariably moralise it and provide role models. There is a fascinated dialectic between the real and realistic fantasy, whereby each seeks fulfilment through absorption in the other. One of the principal agents in the appropriation of the real has been advertising and the principal strategy of marketing has been to redefine reality in terms of a consumerist ideal: no longer does advertising promote a particular product but total lifestyles; their targets, longing for the pure happiness which these images project, eagerly strive for stereotypical status. Such being the strength of this dialectic between the real and realistic fantasy, it is not surprising that hysterical fears are generated around the issue of media control.

Baudrillard has characterised this process as the extinction of reality in *hyperrealism*:

> *Reality itself founders in hyperrealism, the meticulous reduplication of the real, preferably through another, reproductive medium, such as photography…*

> *A possible definition of the real is: that for which it is possible to provide an equivalent representation…… At the conclusion of this process of reproduction, the real becomes not only that which can be reproduced, but that which is always already reproduced: the hyperreal. But*

this does not mean that reality and art are in some sense extinguished through total absorption in one another. Hyperrealism is something like their mutual fulfillment and overflowing into one another through an exchange at the level of simulation of their respective foundational privileges and prejudices…
In fact we must interpret hyperrealism inversely: today, reality itself is hyperrealistic.[7]

In the face of this level of appropriation, a culture of conventional political opposition is — in any radical sense — redundant.

Within the grid established by the physical sciences, the individual subject is further defined by the economic system in terms of 'needs'. Yet these 'needs' are themselves products of the system: Baudrillard —

Needs are not the actuating (mouvante) and original expression of a subject, but the functional reduction of the subject by the system of use value in solidarity with that of exchange value.[8]

This point is particularly important as capitalism's usual self-justification is that the 'free market' responds to the individual's needs and is thereby the ideal instrument for promoting the happiness of the individual. Yet, in practice, the 'free market' has long been abandoned: according to J. K. Galbraith —

… in addition to deciding what the consumer will want and will pay, the firm must take every feasible step to see that what it decides to produce is wanted by the consumer at a remunerative price. And it must see that the labour, materials and equipment that it needs will be available at a cost consistent with the price it will receive. It must exercise control over what is sold. It must exercise control over what is supplied. It must replace the market with planning.[9]

In respect of production, many postmodernist critiques also part company with Marxist thought which has always abetted Capitalism in endorsing production as such. Marxist political economy's point of contact with the individual, the subject, lies in the concept of 'use value' which is postulated over against 'exchange value'; it is, in fact, the crucial referent of the entire system. Yet Marx takes it as being self evident. Baudrillard demonstrates that the concept of use value is an idealisation which provides the 'alibi' for the rest of Marx's political economy.

Every revolutionary perspective today stands or falls on its ability to reinterrogate radically the repressive, reductive, rationalizing metaphysic of utility.[10]

'Utility' (Baudrillard), 'performativity' (Lyotard), 'functionalism', 'accountability' — all watchwords in the current intensification of the economic war — express the essential moral imperatives of our time. The ultimate horror may be that the system no longer needs the discourses that created and sustained it — that it can continue ceaselessly proliferating in an intellectual void — totalitarian and unopposable because, the last vestiges of reality having been destroyed, there exist no possible grounds for opposition. The problem hyperrealism poses for the creators of theatrical, filmic or televisual fictions is that audiences have been conditioned to anticipate and accept as credible an increasingly restricted range of human behaviour. The human has shrunk to the typical and the typical has become the rule. The work's status as fiction facilitates its dismissal on the grounds of being simply unbelievable. While it may be conceded that humans are capable of behaving incredibly, it is not felt that such behaviour has any general relevance.

It is in this respect, however, that some have seen a significant role for Art — one of whose traditional postures has been to oppose 'Life'. Lyotard, for one, lays special stress upon this in a published interview with Brigitte Devismes:

> — *I believe it is absolutely obvious today, and has been for quite some time that, for one thing, the reconstitution of traditional political organisations, even if they present themselves as ultra-leftist organisations is bound to fail, for these settle precisely into the order of the social surface, they are 'recovered', they perpetuate the type of activity the system has instituted as political, they are necessarily alienated, ineffective. The other thing is that all the deconstructions which could appear as aesthetic formalism, 'avant-garde' research, etc., actually make up the only type of activity that is effective, this is because it is functionally — the word is very bad, ontologically would be better and more straightforward — located outside the system; and, by definition, its function is to deconstruct everything that belongs to order, to show that all this 'order' conceals something else, that it represses.*
> *B. D: To show that this order is based on no justifiable authority?*
> — *Yes.*[11]

Lyotard's dissatisfaction with the term 'function' betrays an unease about appearing to prescribe a specific 'role' for the aesthetic, whereas it is the very absence of a function which can enable the aesthetic to evade appropriation. In his examination of the aesthetic in the works of Foucault, Derrida, and Lyotard, David Carroll coins the term paraesthetics for this movement:

> *Paraesthetic critical strategies posit no end to art and no end to theory, because their ends are intricately intertwined and, thus, constantly in question within and outside each. The task of paraesthetic theory is not to resolve all questions concerning the relations of theory with art and literature, but, rather, to rethink these relations and, through the transformation and displacement of art and literature, to recast the philosophical, historical, and political 'fields' — 'fields' with which art and literature are inextricably linked.*[12]

For any art — and we are considering here the question of theatre — the problem of form is crucial. The principal mode of almost all popular television/film/theatre fiction is realism — the simulation of prima facie authenticity. In the light of the theoretical position outlined above it is useless as a vehicle for a radical, critical art. It is, however, the dominant popular form not only in 'democracies' but it is also the only genre with which totalitarian states can feel comfortable; it lends itself easily to academicism — the purveying of 'messages', ideology, role models etc. but one of its chief functions is reassurance: Lyotard —

> *Industrial photography and cinema will be superior to painting and the novel whenever the objective is to stabilise the referent, to arrange it according to a point of view which endows it with a recognisable meaning, to reproduce the syntax and vocabulary which enable the addressee to decipher images and sequences quickly, and so to arrive easily at the consciousness of his own identity as well as the approval which he thereby receives from others — since such structures of images and sequences constitute a communication code among all of them. This is the way the effects of reality, or if one prefers, the fantasies of realism multiply.*[13]

To 'decipher' 'quickly', and 'arrive easily at the consciousness' of one's own 'identity' is, as I will show later, the exact opposite of Seduction which defies interpretation and puts into question the sense of identity. Elsewhere Lyotard argues that a central distinguishing feature of realism is that it seeks to avoid the question of reality. Key features are immediate accessibility and essential conformity with existent values and codes. A good example of this is the way new writers for theatre or television have their work 'shaped' to the requirements of the medium.

> *Under the common name of painting and literature, an unprecedented split is taking place. Those who refuse to reexamine the rules of art pursue successful careers in mass conformism by communicating, by means of the 'correct rules', the endemic desire for reality with objects and situations capable of gratifying it. Pornography is the use of photography and film to such an end. It is becoming a general model for the visual or narrative arts which have not met the challenge of the mass media.*
> *As for the writers who question the rules of plastic and narrative arts and possibly share their suspicions by circulating their work, they are destined to have little credibility in the eyes of those concerned with 'reality' and 'identity'; they have no guarantee of an audience.*[14]

Some leftist theatre practitioners have tended to argue a distinction between 'naturalism' and 'realism' on the basis that the former is imbued with reactionary bourgeois individualist values while the latter presents a progressive socialist perspective. David Edgar, among others, has advocated this form of 'realism':

... the dominant form of television drama is naturalism, which shows people's behaviour as conditioned, primarily or exclusively, by individual and psychological factors. The socialist, on the other hand, requires a form which demonstrates the social and political character of human behaviour.[15]

Edgar sees drama here as a vehicle for ideology and advances the somewhat simplistic notion that whereas the individual and psychology are appropriated, the social and the political are per se oppositional. Edgar's posture, like Bond's (the ideological artist), is essentially academicist: Edgar (the Marxist) knows the truth and Edgar (the dramatist) will undertake to convey this truth to the unknowing via a demonstration (the drama). This position raises a number of questions: why can't the truth be conveyed directly? — why this detour of the demonstration? As a purveyor of truth, there is always the problem that this kind of drama will find itself in the permanent position of being a pale substitute for documentary where the possibilities for 'reality' are so much more impressive — the difference between film of the event itself and the 're-construction with actors'; it can never be more than 'representation'. When drama becomes instrumental in this way, it must tend to lose its experiential integrity and a certain degradation is inevitable. There is also a whole complex of moral dilemmas which pivots around the relationship of those who possess knowledge (and thereby power — e.g. Edgar — ideologist and dramatist with access to communicative media) to those who do not ('the masses' — see quotation below.) It is no longer a matter of conveying 'the truth the whole truth and nothing but the truth' — but rather 'the truths they are capable of absorbing', 'the truths they need to know', truths that will not 'lower their morale at this particularly acute stage of the struggle' etc. The so-called 'elitist' artist does not face this set of problems in that he/she tends to assume dialogue only with equals — i.e. he/she 'communicates' 'irresponsibly', only on his/her own terms: the responsibility of understanding is left with the audience.

Ironically Edgar was forced to admit that this stylistic shift (socio-political realism versus 'psychological' naturalism) was ineffective:

However, in the television age, the masses are so swamped by naturalism and, therefore, by its individualist assumptions, that the superficially similar techniques of realism are incapable of countering individualist ideology. The realist picture of life, with its accurate representations of observable behaviour, is open to constant misinterpretation, however 'typical' the characters, and however total the underlying social context may be.[16]

This somewhat comical agonising was very typical of many proponents of political theatre. It highlights the difficulties which face an ideological art that aspires to anything other than reinforcing the status quo. The realism/naturalism distinction is, at the level of the work itself, meaningless i.e. 'realist' and 'naturalist' productions appear identical. Style is about appearances. As Edgar indicates, the realism/naturalism distinction occurs at the level of interpretation. 'Typical characters' in Socialist dramaturgy become 'stereotypes' when Socialists wish to criticise bourgeois drama. Edgar, however, is clearly in the grip of the 'realist' delusion ('accurate representations of observable behaviour') that realism truly 'reflects' reality — when it is, in fact, as much a system of signs and conventions as any other art form; as I have indicated above, realism is characterised by its forms being so 'conventional', decoding being so rapid and easy, that its signs appear transparent.

Brecht was well aware of realism's problems as a radical artistic genre and indeed, with his alienation theory, he seems to have gone to considerable lengths in the opposite direction: audiences are to be continually alerted to the fact that the representation they are witnessing is *not* real. Brecht's objections to realism were that audiences used it as a vehicle for escapism, or simply marvelled at the virtuosity of its authenticity. Where his critique intersects with Lyotard's, lies in their awareness of the reassuring, anodyne effect of realism — it does not encourage a critical state of mind — and he claimed to avoid the simplistic totalitarian audience relation of Social (ist) Realism by forcing a critical stance upon the audience through the use of alienatory devices.

Brecht's rationalism, however, performs the same controlling function as Bond's or as Edgar's Marxism — it is, theoretically, the organising principle of his artistic method. When Brecht succeeds in adhering to his ideological purpose, his representational 'experiments' are rigged so that any open critical response from his audience is circumvented. All Brecht's fuss with anti-realist, anti-illusionist devices suggests nothing so much as the typical conjuror's posturings of persistently demonstrating empty hands, showing the inside of the top hat, revealing both sides of the handkerchief etc. The implication is that we see everything, no concealment, no tricks — we are in touch with 'reality' throughout — all of which serves to facilitate the foisting of an 'illusion'.

Thus in *The Life of Galileo*, Brecht represents the confrontation between Galileo and the Catholic Church as symbolic of the 'historic' struggle between Science and Religion, progress and reaction, Truth and Falsehood. I cite this play because it seems to be widely revered as a 'classic' throughout the British theatrical establishment receiving frequent productions, one of which in 1980 at the National Theatre was numbered amongst their 'biggest and costliest ventures.'[17]. The 'great' scientist is presented in the ideologically acceptable stereotype of 'the genius', but the principle alienation effect of the play lies in portraying him as an anti-hero: he is selfish, greedy, dishonest, arrogant and cowardly. In short, the audience are invited to criticise everything about Galileo except his science. Brecht, who acclaimed himself 'the Einstein of the new stage form',[18] states in his notes on Scene 14:

> *What needs to be altered is the popular conception of heroism, ethical precepts and so on. The one thing that counts is one's contribution to science, and so forth.*[19]

Much emphasis, therefore, is laid on Galileo's 'brilliance' and his role as a populariser of science by writing not in elitist Latin but ordinary Italian:

> *I am still blamed for once having written an astronomical work in the language of the market place.*[20]

Of this particular work, 'Dialogo Sopra i Due Massimi Sistemi del Mondo', Koestler, in his account of the 'historical' Galileo in *The Sleepwalkers* says:

> *It is true that Galileo was writing for a lay audience, and in Italian; his account however, was not a simplification but a distortion of the facts, not popular science, but misleading propaganda.*[21]

And Stillman Drake, translator and biographer of Galileo:

> *A drastic simplification of Copernicus may have seemed to him an easier didactic device. This is, at least, the charitable hypothesis. But the problem remains of how Galileo could commit the capital error, against which he had warned others so many time, of constructing theories in defiance of the best results of observation.*[22]

In contradistinction to Brecht's version, the actual 'Dialogue' of Galileo, which precipitated his trial, attempts to 'prove' the Copernican heliocentric system by an incorrect argument based on tidal movement — which is unscientific in so far as it flies in the face of observable facts (there are two tides a day not one). He contradicts himself concerning the tilt in the axes of rotating bodies and rejects as superstition Kepler's correct explanation of tidal behaviour. Koestler sums up this 'popular' treatise thus:

> *The truth is that after his sensational discoveries in 1610, Galileo neglected both observational research and astronomic theory in favour of his propaganda crusade. By the time he wrote the 'Dialogue' he had lost touch with new developments in that field, and had forgotten even what Copernicus had said.*[23]

In fact, there was no essential reason why the church needed to be committed to the defense of the geocentric model — other than the fact that Galileo appears to have gone out of his way to provoke offense among the clergy: Catholicism had successfully shifted its position on the sphericity of the earth. Recent research has suggested that the heliocentric/geocentric controversy was a 'cover' for more serious objections to Galileo which hinged on his espousal of atomism, a theory inconsistent with the belief in trans-substantiation; this, of course, hit at the heart of Catholic doctrine.[24] Brecht, however, presents a rigorously empirical, 'doubting' Galileo, who challenges all forms of dogma which conflict with his observation of the facts and his reason. What is therefore idealised and shielded from critical appraisal in Brecht's portrait is Galileo the 'Scientist' and 'Science' itself. He achieves this, like his hero, by ignoring or distorting the evidence available to make it fit his ideological preconceptions, covering up this manoeuvre by distracting the audience with his 'alienation' of Galileo qua bourgeois individualist hero.

One of the most unfortunate aspects of the Brechtian rational theatre has been the influence of its 'theory' — especially in Britain. In particular, his schematised generalisations of the 'two-legs-good: four-legs-bad' variety, became cliches not only of the liberal/left theatrical consensus but also of Theatre Studies pedagogy in educational establishments. This kind of thing —

DRAMATIC FORM OF THEATRE	*EPIC FORM OF THEATRE*
Plot	*Narrative*
Implicates the spectator in	*Turns the spectator into*
a stage situation and	*an observer but*
wears down his power of action	*arouses his power of action*
the human being is taken	*the human being is the object*
for granted	*of the enquiry*
he is unalterable	*he is alterable and able to alter*
eyes on the finish	*eyes on the course*
one scene makes another	*each scene for itself*
growth	*montage*
etc.	*etc.*[25]

The main distinction between these two forms is the organising principle of the narrator who structures events for the audience via montage and is therefore in a position to unify and resolve contradictions. In dramatic form, there is no narrator, only participants; the structuring principle can only be immanent development from a given scenario — not necessarily growth, it could be decay. This is what Barker means when he talks, in respect of *Claw*, of withdrawing himself from the action. The drama then relies on the conflict of irreducible opposites and, on the strength of this, would appear to be less of a propaganda medium than Epic. And of course propaganda aims to arouse its targets to action. One of the most damaging examples of this tendency of leftist thought to simplistic categorisations has been the individual/collectivity opposition whereby the former concept has been denigrated in favour of the latter (see David Edgar above); the effect of this has been to allow the forces of political reaction to represent themselves as championing the individual in the mythically enshrined form of the choosing producer/consumer.

While therefore Barker's aesthetic, and — as I intend to show — his practice, have been consonant with the most radical trends in Postmodernist thinking, the immediate context of the liberal/left British theatrical establishment has been characterised by a phase of extreme artistic conservatism. This is reflected not only in the supposely 'progressive' Brecht/Bond ideal of a Rational Theatre but is further manifest in the wide currency of mechanically rationalistic performance techniques such as those advocated by Stanislavsky.

In the light of deconstruction, I have indicated some of the central problems of contemporary theatrical practice through a consideration of the major mode of artistic production — realism and the critical realism of Brecht. Though the term 'deconstruction' can be frequently encountered in critical writings about theatre, it is rarely employed in the sense I have implied above: more usually it signifies the substitution of 'truth' in place of 'myth' — socialist truths for capitalist lies. Radical deconstruction, however, rejects the truth/falsehood dialectic. Critical activity is carried on not by positing an alternative ideological 'position', rather discourses are turned against themselves in a movement of pure inversion or are employed against each other to effect their mutual destruction. To 'demythologise' — the declared aim of much political theatre — is not, strictly speaking, to deconstruct because, against the myth, it postulates a reality/truth value — 'this it how it really was/is'. If one does not share the ideological perspective of the demythologiser, then one myth has merely been substituted for another — as in *The Life of Galileo*. If reality itself has been appropriated by the exchange-value system, the extent to which this might comprise a valid oppositional strategy is open to doubt. It may be objected that such apparently 'value-free' deconstructive strategies are nihilistic and purely destructive but deconstruction can be positive in that it comprises a continuous movement of intellectual liberation. The deconstruction of authoritative discourses opens up a space in which desire can perpetually reinscribe itself anew. By liberation, I mean, the process of freeing humans from deterministic notions such as historical, social or biological conditioning — what Blake referred to as 'mind-forged manacles'.

It is perhaps not too fanciful to compare our situation today to the period of the Renaissance: in the collapse of the Medieval Christian 'world' we can glimpse the current collapse of the 'world' of scientific reason. In both cases, a space opens up in which the nature of the human once more becomes an issue and a possiblity. In this regard, Peter Szondi's description of the 'project' of the 'Modern Drama' could offer an appropriate contemporary poetics of the theatre:

> The Drama of modernity came into being in the Renaissance. It was the result of a bold intellectual effort made by a newly self-conscious being who, after the collapse of the medieval worldview, sought to create an artistic reality within which he could fix and mirror himself **on the basis of interpersonal relationships alone**.[26] (my emphasis)

Szondi sees the drama as a device for providing a perspective on the human. Particularly important is the relegation of the world of objects:

> Most radical of all was the exclusion of that which could not express itself — the world of objects — unless it entered the realm of interpersonal relations.[27]

In the case of the contemporary world, such an exclusion would encompass objects like the authoritative discourses discussed above. For Szondi the dramatic world proper is a world of subjective and inter-subjective expression:

> By deciding to disclose himself to this contemporary world, man transformed his internal being into a palpable and dramatic presence.[28]

The term 'dis-closure' focusses effectively the difference between Szondi's Drama (which I would argue is also Barker's) and the dramaturgy of a Brecht, a Bond or an Edgar. The former aims at *disclosure* — an opening, an expression which assumes a continuation of dialogue and likewise a continuation of the process of meaning. The latter aims at closure — the purpose of the play is to convey a pre-determined set of fixed ideas — arrested meaning. Szondi's drama is radically heuristic and exploratory. The view that the dramatist who eschews ideological commitment must of necessity be in the grip of an ideology is per se an ideological view. Where a dramatist is ideologically committed and feels the need to convey his/her views, then this will generally be the least *dramatic* part of the work; we are all familiar with those moments when characters obviously become mouthpieces — when there is not an equivalent element of contradiction in the drama.

> The dramatist is absent from the Drama. He does not speak; he institutes discussion. The Drama is not written, it is set. All the lines spoken in the Drama are dis-closures. They are

spoken in context and remain there. They should in no way be perceived as coming from the author.[29]

In short, according to Szondi, nothing is 'authorised'. It may be objected that this overt absence of the author/creator is merely a formal absence, that he/she by 'pulling the strings' of the characters, consciously or subconsciously is still conveying a view laden with consequent ideological values; the absence of a narrator merely serving to conceal the communication of such 'messages', thereby communicating them all the more effectively. And of course, it is a favoured critical game to find evidence in the text which 'proves' such ideological biases. But these are of course 'readings' and the fact that, in the case of sophisticated texts certainly, such readings can be many and contradictory would tend to counter the assertion that all texts are intrinsically ideological. If it is possible to advance widely different political readings of a text, — to what extent can one claim that the text itself is 'value-laden'? On the other hand where there is a narraator to communicate the authorial view — as, for example, in certain plays by Brecht and Bond — the possibilities for diverse readings are correspondingly discouraged.

For Szondi, the Drama does not seek to 'reflect' or re-present 'reality'; it is itself and happens always in the present. For this reason, audiences should not distinguish performers from roles — as prescribed by Brecht. Lear is not a representation of Lear — he is, uniquely, Lear. Because the 'real' world is admitted only in so far as elements of it are filtered through the characters, then authoritative discourses are only perceived as objects of human consciouness — created, sustained and discarded through those consciousnesses. The individual subject is primary — all the rest is secondary. This relegation of the external enables the drama to generate its own movement — an element which is identical to Aristotle's recommendation of unity of action.

Barker's plays have increasingly tended in the direction of this model. His most recently produced work, *Hated Nightfall* (1994), preserves entirely the three so-called Aristotelian unities. He has stated that he does not plan what he writes and does not know how the action he is engaged in at any one time will turn out. A group of characters are presented along with a scenario which they then proceed to work out. The scenario is invariably 'distanced' both for the audience and the characters themselves, — usually the circumstances are either catastrophic or immediately post- catastrophic, because, as I have already suggested, such ruptures conveniently dispose of the normalising, reassuring, socially enforced patterns of daily existence which we take for 'reality'.

The dialectical, relational character of this dramatic model must necessarily express itself in the dialogue; language, therefore, is of primary importance and, according to Szondi, takes precedence over all the other elements of production. As such, it must accept the burden of responsibility for the anti-realistic project of the drama and a stylised, poetic speech is essential. Other aspects such as the visual are subordinate to language and their function is to situate and clarify speech. The Brechtian notion of 'gestus' where utterance is merely part of a dramatic totality occupies a less significant role in such a poetic dramaturgy. In fact, the whole notion of 'languages' of the body or of design needs to be treated with considerable circumspection. Language is unique and no other system of signs is remotely equivalent to it. The problem with 'gestus' is that it is appropriated and belongs essentially to hyperreality. It is possible to 'play' with 'gestus': Handke does so in *The Ride Across Lake Constance* but the effect of this is merely to expose the aporia of realism and the real. If language is the fundamental structuring process of human experience, then any fundamental reorganisation of that experience must occur at the linguistic level. The process of this stylisation works to defamiliarise reality by exposing the medium (language) to consciousness: Tony Bennett —

> *Literature characteristically works on and subverts those linguistic, perceptual and cognitive forms which conventionally condition our access to **reality** itself. Literature thus effects a twofold shift of perceptions. For what it makes appear strange is not merely the 'reality' which has been distanced from habitual modes of representation but also those habitual modes of representation themselves. Literature offers not only a new insight into 'reality' but also reveals the formal operations whereby what is commonly taken for 'reality' is constructed.*[30]

Those, therefore, along with Artaud, who have insisted strongly on the separation of theatre from literature, arguing that the former possesses its own 'language', have tended towards the reduction of its most radically subversive aspect — articulate speech. There is, in fact, a firmly established tradition in the post-War British theatre of an inarticulate or deficient speech which has the general effect of rendering the speaker 'transparent'. The plays of Pinter suggest themselves as, perhaps, the most salient example of this kind of dialogue and the extent to which it can be exploited for dramatic effect. In plays like *Abigail's Party* by Mike Leigh, however, the inarticulacy becomes positively garrulous: the characters talk incessantly but say nothing. Their utterance is pure neurotic behaviourism which dramatises their incapacity for any genuine interaction. Bond's *Saved* takes inarticulacy to extreme lengths: Scene One of the play is fairly typical — the average length of line comprises 4.2 words; only two words in the entire scene exceed two syllables; the final scene — involving four characters in a domestic interior —

contains a single line of four words in three pages of detailed stage directions: language has become altogether redundant. The characters' inarticulacy reflects entrapment in their situation — they are doomed to futile repetitions with their escape routes blocked by pernicious chunks of ideology which have been absorbed unchallenged and acquired the status of self-evident truths. As Martin Esslin said of *Saved*:

> ... *their very speechlessness is made to yield communication, we can look right inside their narrow, confined, limited and pathetic emotional world.*[31]

Obviously, this kind of transparency is very much in accordance with the Brechtian aim of demonstrating the socially conditioned nature of human behaviour. What enthralled Esslin, however, Barker found repugnant:

> *SAVED was one of the first plays I ever saw in the theatre — and I myself was not a writer then. So I suppose that seeing the life of my own class and background could be represented on the stage made me want to write a play — and, perhaps, write it better. I do remember feeling that Bond's presentation of the South London working class was abominable and contemptuous. The inarticulacy, the grunting and the monosyllabics, being accepted as a portrayal of working class people did offend me and may have inspired me to write CHEEK which did lend articulacy to the characters.*[32]

The whole focus, however, of the Royal Court 'house style' was to direct attention away from speech and its seductions towards action. One of the regular actors at the Court during this period was Jack Shepherd:

> *During the period when I worked intensively at the Court a defined way of rehearsing the actors was in the process of being evolved... A good actor was someone who could draw attention to the thing that was said, as opposed to the way it was being spoken. Naturalness, not naturalism. Altruism, not egotism. And above all, in rehearsal, there was no substitute for doing. As Bill Gaskill repeatedly said: 'Don't talk about it — do it.' And much more.*
> *What made it difficult was that a lot of the theory tended to run right across the grain of an actor's instinct. It was very hard to find a synthesis.*[33]

Apart from the fact that the literary element is essential to the tradition of European drama and to refuse literature is to refuse engagement with that tradition, the anti-literature lobby tend to confuse matters by advancing the argument that while words are clearly the medium of literature, action is the proper medium of drama. This ignores the fact that most acts which may be said to carry dramatic significance are speech acts. When Aristotle emphasises that tragedy is essentially 'action', it is for the purposes of defining it over against epic which involves 'reportage' (narration). Δρᾶν, (dran) whence 'drama' is derived, Aristotle informs us,[34] is the Doric equivalent of the Attic verb πράττειν (prattein); the primary meaning of this ubiquitous lexical item is 'to pass through'[35]. It would appear that Aristotle's distinction is between events which are happening **now** and events which are being reported — the present and the past tense; both, however, are speech events. His conception of drama as an essentially linguistic phenomenon is made clear in his discussion of the elements of tragedy where spectacle and music are relegated to the end of the list:

> *Of the remaining pleasurable elements, the music is the most important, and the spectacle, however seductive, is the crudest and least germane to the poetry.* **For the power of tragedy exists independently of performance and actors...** (My emphasis)[36]

And again later, when he argues the superiority of tragedy to epic:

> *Also tragedy can achieve its effect without movement — just as well as epic — since its qualities are apparent from reading it.*[37]

Doubtless, when Aristotle talks of reading, he would be thinking of reading aloud. The principal argument against tragedy which he is anxious to deflect here is that tragedy depends upon the 'vulgar' element of spectacle because —

> *Epic is said to appeal to cultivated readers who do not need the help of visible forms...*[38]

In fact, Aristotle accepts the argument that the 'realisation' of the text is a debasement but counters the criticism by saying that this element is not essential. The fundamental distinction between the epic and the dramatic lies, not in the ascription of performance to the latter, but in the figure of the narrator — present in the epic, absent in the dramatic. The epic is the narrative organisation of past events — the principle of organisation is a single viewpoint (the narrator's, a 'worldview'). Drama is organised in the present around irreducible conflict — there is no ultimate reconciliation in a universe which is inexorably chaotic. This is what makes the drama with its agonistic relativism and unqualified acceptance of the other, a more appropriate postmodernist art form than the didactic and totalitarian epic.

Aristotle's contempt for performance is excessive and no doubt reflects the inferior standards of the theatre in his own day which was reduced to the depressingly familiar practice of 'rejuvenating' classics with gimmickry. It is doubtful whether Aeschylus, Sophocles or Euripides would have shared his aversion but it is equally certain that they would have rejected any notion of a theatre which decentred the poetic text. Barker's emphasis on literary style which contrasts sharply with the 'theatre of inarticulacy' as expressed most notably in Bond's *Saved* or numerous other dramas of working class life, — should not be seen therefore as 'untheatrical' but rather as restoring language to its rightful pre-eminence in a theatre which aspires to the status of a radical art form.

I have attempted to argue that Barker's use of the dramatic form is uniquely appropriate to the anti-ideological, deconstructivist moment in that it presents a decentred, purely relational world which goes beyond the quiescent fantasies of realism without the support of any authorising discourses. What does support Barker's aesthetic discourse? Or is it — as Derrida[39] asserts all literature should be (in every sense of the word) — 'insupportable'? The problem with the outright rejection of realism is that what most people regard as their direct experience is structured by Baudrillard's 'hyperrealism'. This is why much avant-garde art can appear totally alienating; it bears no resemblance to 'lived' experience. Ortega y Gasset complains of this 'dehumanization':

> *By divesting them of their element of 'lived' reality, the artist has blown up the bridges and burnt the ships that could have taken us back to our daily world.*[40]

In the case of drama, however, the problem of apparent dehumanisation can be overcome through the actors, who need to 'live' their roles with the same degree of total absorption and conviction as demanded by Stanislavsky; albeit Barker's characters function according to a significantly different 'rationale'. The alienation occasioned by the anti-realistic style can thereby be counteracted, though not negated, by the very 'human' interactions between the characters. The actors' 'total immersion' in their roles should serve to **seduce** the audience into the emotional life of the plays. In all of this the key concept is **seduction**; **seduction** is the 'rationale' or 'non-rationale'; it is the play of subjects in which the subject disappears; **seduction** is more significant to Barker's dramaturgy than alienation is to Brecht's.

2

SEDUCTION

From the moment that we place desire on the side of acquisition, we make desire an idealistic (dialectical, nihilistic) conception, which causes us to look upon it as primarily a lack: a lack of an object, a lack of the real object...
Desire does not lack anything; it does not lack its object. It is, rather, the subject that is missing in desire, or desire that lacks a fixed subject; there is no fixed subject unless there is repression. Desire and its object are one and the same thing...
Deleuze & Guattari: ANTI-OEDIPUS[1]

In so far as it presents a deflection which all forms of truth-based discourse must repress, seduction is a concept frequently encountered in deconstructive readings. In normal parlance it is associated, almost exclusively, with calculated attempts to obtain sexual favours. In deconstruction the scope of the term is both wider and more precise. Baudrillard, however, begins his essay 'On Seduction' thus:

Seduction is that which extracts meaning from discourse and detracts it from its truth.[2]

Under which circumstances, repression or resistance might appear perfectly reasonable or legitimate. However, deconstructive discourse is concerned to interrogate what we mean by 'reason', 'legitimacy' and — above all — 'truth'. Particularly problematical is the question of authority and Jacques Derrida has advanced a critique of the Western philosophical 'logos' — from Plato to Lacan — which demonstrates how the logos — essentially a chain of writings — grounds itself in a conception of truth as a self-evident or transparent speech. Derrida traces this tradition back to the Socratic dialogues where truth is described as 'a writing in the soul', the revelation of which is imparted via the speech of an authorised teacher to genuine disciples — the original seduction. This notion of truth is related to Derrida's critique of the much more insidious, ubiquitous illusion of self-presence which haunts Western discourses: the notion that things have an identity in and of themselves — an objective reality. Derrida's critique derives from Heidegger's attempt to reconstitute the original structure of being through an etymological scrutiny of the different verbal forms of the concept (Sein —

dasein — 'being'). However, where Heidegger perceives a semantic plurality which nevertheless combines to form a meaningful 'original' totality (Heidegger claims to retrieve the 'truth' about being), Derrida perceives a diverse group of signifiers which have drifted together into an arbitrary concept which has established the central problematics of Western thought without being interrogated itself. According to Saussure, language signifies through a system of difference — a lexical item has no meaning in itself, no plenitude; it only defines itself in relation to the system of linguistic difference of which it is a part. In spite of his own argument, Saussure continues to defer to the notion of self-presence derived from phonetic speech in the incorporation within his system of the 'signified' and the 'referent' which infer the independent existence of a 'world' separate from language. According to Derrida, this conception of meaningful self-presence derives from the 'moment' of utterance when language can appear transparent in the light of thought (Cogito ergo sum). Any form of language, however, consists of signs which refer elsewhere and, although speech can appear transparent, when considered within the frame of a general semiology, it loses this privilege. This comprises one of the most significant claims advanced by Derrida: specifically that the whole of our epistemology consists of a writing which clings to an illusion of an immanent, self-present meaning ultimately derived from speech.

Derrida reverses this hierarchy and regards speech as a form of writing. His most important concept in characterising the operation of writing is 'differance'. This could be seen as fabricated in antithesis to 'being' (in the sense of self-presence): this coinage subsumes the Saussurian concept of difference as constitutive of meaning but also incorporates the semantic range of the word 'defer" — especially in the sense of 'putting off/delaying' and 'acknowledging authority'. In fact, Derrida's linguistic and philosophical views are analogous to developments in twentieth century physics with the Newtonian universe framed in an Absolute Space and an Absolute Time giving way to a general relativity where phenomena exist solely in relation to an observer or observers (i.e. they exist only 'referentially').

This substitution of differance for self-presence is not the only reversal with regard to deconstructive readings of written texts; there are numerous other discursive practices clustered around this same linguistic nexus of 'truth'/'self-presence' which require critical scrutiny. For example, there is the 'literal'/'metaphorical' antithesis; the former term has been conventionally 'privileged' as a 'proper' or 'true' adequation of a term to its referent, while the latter has been relegated to the status of decorative artifice. Yet, from a diachronic perspective, metaphoricity is fundamental to the development of a language — i.e. historically all words are metaphors, — though whether they overtly present themselves as such is a different matter. The 'literal' effect, which is closely linked to transparency, is invariably the product of a 'superficial' reading — which, for practical purposes, is all that most forms of reading require. It does not, however, 'exhaust' any text — as twentieth century hermeneutics demonstrates.

I have referred to 'truth' in terms of Derrida's conception of self-present meaning but I wish to enlarge upon the semantic range of the word as it figures quite significantly in this discourse by way of antithesis to seduction. For Heidegger, whose whole philosophic enterprise involved recovering an authentic knowledge of 'being' from its fallen contemporary state, truth was not confined to mere 'adaequatio' (equivalence of words and things). The ancient Greek word for truth αλήθεια, he etymologised as α — λήθεια: the α prefix meaning 'not' and ληθεια being derived from the verb λανθάνειν usually translated into English as 'to lie hidden'. He therefore conceived of 'truth' as essentially associated with 'unconcealment'. Heidegger related this to 'appearances' (φαινόμενα- phenomena); a φαινόμενον, however, was not 'mere appearance' but according to Heidegger:

> … *appearance… does not mean showing itself; it means rather the announcing-itself by something which does not show itself, but which announces itself through something which does show itself.*[3]

The 'truth-based discourse' 'reads' all phenomena in this way and attempts to penetrate to the law or organising principle behind appearances; this is a question of authority, of control. Even psychoanalytic discourse which can subvert manifest discourse does so in the interests of apprehending the 'truth' of the former. Baudrillard —

> *Interpretation is that which, shattering appearances and the play of manifest discourse, will set meaning free by remaking connections with latent discourse.*
> *In seduction, conversely, it is somehow the manifest discourse, the most 'superficial' aspect of discourse, which acts upon the underlying prohibition (conscious or unconscious) in order to nullify it and substitute for it the charms and traps of appearances. Appearances, which are not at all frivolous, are the site of play and chance taking the site of a passion for diversion — to seduce signs here is far more important than the emergence of any truth.*[4]

Baudrillard advances the theoretical hypothesis that seduction is the ultimate 'reality' in the sense that it encompasses all 'truth' discourses — the image and paradigm of which he sees in the process of Production. It is to this area that he directs the polemical weight of his discourse:

Everything is seduction and nothing but seduction.
They wanted us to believe that everything was production. The leitmotiv of
world transformation, the play of productive forces is to regulate the flow of things.
Seduction is merely an immoral, frivolous, superficial and superfluous process: one within the
realm of signs and appearances; one that is devoted to pleasure and the usufruct of useless
bodies…
Production merely accumulates and is never diverted from its end. It replaces all illusion with
just one: its own, which has become the reality principle. Production, like the revolution, puts
an end to the epidemic of appearances. But seduction is inevitable.[5]

The world of production must repress the action of seduction, marginalise it, trivialise it or reduce it; seduction's potency is evidenced in its persistence — in spite of an apparently all powerful rationality, it will not be exterminated. It is in the light of seduction theory, bearing in mind Derrida's conception of discursive 'truth' as deferring ultimately to a self-present speech, that I wish to consider the theatrical moment.

There is a final issue relating to the fundamental structures of the Western 'logos' and the various truth-based discourses it has spawned which seems to me to be of particular importance with reference to Barker's plays and to the drama in general — especially according to the theoretical model postulated by Szondi in *The Theory of the Modern Drama*. This particular critique achieves its most articulate expression in the work of Emmanuel Levinas.[6] Levinas argues that the 'logos', from its Greek origins — especially Plato and Aristotle, has constituted itself on authoritarian lines; it has been concerned with power, comprehension, 'grasping' — above all, the reduction of the Other to the same. The traditional theoretical polarities of subject and object comprise the essential relationship of this thought. As the project of reason is to eliminate the Other and reduce it to Same, it finds itself haunted by a curious solitude with thinkers frequently having to fend off the imputation of solipsism. For Levinas, however, the accusation is apt:

Solipsism is neither observation nor sophism; it is the very structure of reason.[7]

The alternative relation proposed by Levinas is of a desire which is respect and knowledge of the other **as other.** Derrida expresses the relation thus:

Neither theoretical intentionality nor the affectivity of need exhaust the movement of desire:
they have as their meaning and end their own accomplishment, their own fulfillment and
satisfaction within the totality and identity of the same. Desire, on the contrary, permits itself
to be appealed to by the absolutely irreducible exteriority of the other to which it must remain
infinitely inadequate. Desire is equal only to excess. No totality will ever encompass it. Thus,
the metaphysics of desire is a metaphysics of infinite separation…Here there is no return. For
desire is not unhappy. It is opening and freedom.[8]

This is an **ethical** relation; an ontology founded not in the subject-object polarisation but in the subject-other. Nor is this what conventional metaphysics would term intersubjectivity which is an essentially solipsistic reason's concession towards other — the concession that certain existents which are primarily object for me are, for themselves, subjects like me; this can be subject to a variety to ethnic, religious, sexual, species qualifications. Such a concession is merely an extension of the process of reification to comprehend and assimilate the other to the same. It is to those non–authoritarian modes of relating to and knowing the other, marginalised and repressed by the power discourses of our social institutions, that Barker's drama returns us and Baudrillard's essay 'On Seduction' points a finger. This is not to say that Barker does not concern himself with authority — obviously power relations are of central importance, particularly where they intersect with the personal. The point is that relations of whatever character are not mediated through 'authorised' discourses — i.e. they are not structured in accordance with these by the dramatist.

This includes social 'morality'; ethics cannot be reduced to a system of abstract and universal dos and don'ts. Levinas:

> *The fixed point cannot be some incontestable 'truth', a 'certain' statement that would always be subject to psychoanalysis; it can only be the absolute status of an interlocutor, a being, and not of a truth about beings. An interlocutor is not affirmed like a truth, but believed. This faith or trust does not designate here a second source of cognition, but is presupposed by every theoretical statement. Faith is not the knowledge of a truth open to doubt or capable of being certain; it is something outside of those modalities, it is the face to face encounter with a hard and substantial interlocutor who is the origin of himself, already dominating the forces which constitute him and sway him, a you, arising inevitably, solid and noumenal, behind the man known in that bit of absolutely decent skin which is the face, which closes over the nocturnal chaos and opens upon what it can take up and for which it can answer.*[9]

Barker's ethical position takes the relation with the other as its focus. In *That Good Between Us*, the action of the drama shows a Britain descending into the nightmare of a police state. The key aspect of this decline is not this or that political agenda or ideology, but the readiness of individuals to sacrifice all the affective ties and bonds of interpersonal relations in the interests of furthering or preserving their own status as defined by power or ideology. 'That good between us' **is** the 'faith or trust' that Levinas refers to above and which is, according to him, the foundation of morality. Similarly in *The Unforseen Consequences of a Political Act*, one of *The Possibilities*, Judith insists that her killing of Holofernes was 'a crime' because she spoke desire to him.[10] The fact that she has saved her race, that Holofernes was a military butcher about to massacre them all, is neither here nor there and cannot mitigate or abate her personal guilt. When Barker talks of restoring to the theatre the task of moral speculation, it would appear that his concern is to investigate what happens to individuals who commit themselves to particular courses of action or strategies — very often conventional transgressions or violations. In this sense his characters are usually explorers who are not content to live their lives within the parameters of received social wisdom and morality. Their dilemmas are resolved not by reference to social norms but instinctively.

I have tried to suggest, very briefly, some of the ways in which truth–based discourses have been problematised. As I hope to demonstrate, *on the one hand,* Barker's texts in their divergence from 'truth/reality/authenticity' principles actively call these into question; *on the other*, the major acting and production discourses employed in contemporary theatre actively pursue these very principles — Stanislavsky, Brecht, Grotowski et al deploy the 'jargon of authenticity' to an extent, it could be argued, that they depend on it. I believe that this has led to difficulties in staging Barker's plays.

Baudrillard essays to describe some of the processes of seduction and I shall outline these here because it will be necessary to refer to them when I consider Barker's texts. It will be appreciated that the 'irrational' nature of these elements means that they do not, at first sight, easily cohere in an orderly and summarisable form. The first, and perhaps the most important concept is the secret.

> *The secret: the seductive and initiatory quality of that which cannot be said because it is meaningless, and of that which is not said even though it gets around. Hence I know the other's secret but do not reveal it, and he knows I know it but does not let it be acknowledged: the intensity between the two is simply the secret of the secret.*[11]

Common sense thinking tends to equate the secret retrospectively with the 'thing concealed' and that's that. In focussing on the thing, it fails to acknowledge the process, for when the secret is known, it is, by definition, no longer secret. Baudrillard's point is that the secret exercises a fascination, a power which both manifest discourse and psychological discourse tend only to invest in palpable objects. The secret can operate in many ways. Baudrillard asserts, for instance, that the pope, the grand inquisitor and the great Jesuits or theologians knew that God did not exist and that this secret was their secret strength, the foundation of their power. Similarly, in discussing how 'trompe–1'oeil' exposes 'reality' through an apparent excess of reality, he cites the trompe–1'oeil studiolos of the Duke of Urbino, Frederigo da Montefeltre, in the ducal palaces of Urbino and Gubbio. Baudrillard argues that these spaces are a 'reverse microcosm' where space is actualised in simulation; this exposes the 'secret' of the ducal power:

> *A complete reversal of the rules of the game is in effect here, one which would ironically lead us to think that, through the allegory of the trompe–1'oeil, the external space of the palace and beyond it to the city, as well as the political space, the actual locus of power, would perhaps be nothing more than a perspective effect. Such a dangerous secret, such a radical hypothesis, the Prince must keep to himself, within himself, in strict secrecy: for it is in fact the secret of his power.*
>
> *Since Machiavelli politicians have perhaps always known that the mastery of simulated space is the source of power, that the political is not a real activity or space, but a simulation model, whose manifestations are simply achieved effects.[12]*

A further example of the seductive power of the secret cited by Baudrillard is to be found in Kierkegaard's *'Diary of a Seducer'*. A young girl is perceived as an enigma; to seduce her, the seducer must in turn become an enigma to her. The seduction resolves the affair without disclosing the secret. It could be argued that the 'true' meaning was sexuality, yet there was nothing in the place where others might have deduced sex: Baudrillard —

> *And this nothing of the secret, this unsignified of seduction circulates, flows beneath words and meaning, faster than meaning: it is what affects you before utterances reach you, in the time it takes for them to vanish. Seduction beneath discourse is invisible; from sign to sign, it remains a secret circulation.[13]*

Baudrillard insists that there is no active and passive in seduction - no subject and object. Within the framework of rationalist causality, seduction evidences itself as the irruption of the irrational, operating instantaneously in a single movement which is its own end. In order to seduce, it is necessary that one be seduced oneself; being seduced is very seductive. The challenge is illuminating in this respect:

> *To challenge or seduce is always to drive the other mad, but in a mutual vertigo: madness from the vertiginous absence that unites them, and from their mutual involvement. Such is the inevitability of the challenge, and consequently the reason why we cannot help but respond to it: for it inaugurates a kind of mad relation, quite different from communication and exchange; a dual relation transacted by meaningless signs, but connected by a fundamental rule and its secret observance. The challenge terminates all contracts, all exchanges regulated by law (the law of nature or the law of value) and substitutes for it a highly conventional and ritualised pact. An unremitting obligation to respond and outdo, governed by a fundamental rule of the game, and proceeding according to its own rhythm. Contrary to the law which is always written in stone, in the heart, or in the sky, this fundamental rule never needs to be stated; it must never be stated. It is immediate, immanent, and inevitable (whereas the law is transcendental and explicit).[14]*

I have quoted this paragraph in full because it describes several important aspects of the processes of seduction — challenge, the duel relation, vertigo, madness, the suspension of 'normal' constraints and the substitution of a pact, the obligation to exceed. All of these are of particular importance in 'reading' Barker's plays and understanding the apparently irrational behaviour of his characters. Another significant aspect of the dual relation is the bluff which often amounts to fooling oneself in order to fool the other. This is implicit in Baudrillard's statement:

> To seduce is to die as reality and reconstitute oneself as illusion. It is to be taken in by one's own illusion and move in an enchanted world.[15]

> The strategy of seduction is one of deception. It lies in wait for all that tends to confuse itself with reality.[16]

These assertions also have clear implications for the business of acting.

Seduction goes further than this in its contravention of power/reason. Baudrillard asserts that it annihilates power relations not only because to seduce is to weaken but because we seduce **with weakness:**

> We seduce with our death, with our vulnerability, and with the void that haunts us.[17]

Seduction is never a matter of using strength. Once initiated seduction offers the permanent possibility of total reversal; this is part of its charm and its risk. Indeed reversal is fundamental to seductive strategy in that it comprises an essential energy source: the challenge is the catalyst for turning the 'dead weight' of prohibition, custom, the law, the proper etc. through a reversal into weightless energy. Aristotle, of course, sets 'reversal' (περιπέτεια) at the very heart of dramatic structure and perhaps it was the seduction of this that created the sense of 'catharsis'.

One of the most obvious convergences of Baudrillard with Barker is in respect of the dead. Baudrillard:

> They are only dead when echoes no longer reach them from this world to seduce them, and rituals no longer defy them to exist.
> To us, only those who no longer produce are dead. In reality, only those who do not wish to seduce, nor be seduced, are dead.[18]

The dead abound in Barker's plays. Barker:

> An ugly struggle goes on over the dead. They beckon to the living because their 'sacrifice' (which it never is) is employed to justify further 'sacrifice'. They are forever calling more people 'over'.[19]

In the 'world' of seduction, the dead can be very much alive. The etymology of the Ancient Greek word for seduction — ψυχαγωγεῖν (psychagogein) — is interesting in this respect since the primary meanings cited in the lexicon (Liddell and Scott) are 'to be a conductor of the dead', 'to evoke or conjure up the dead'.

One of the most insistent assertions Barker makes is that the individual is not finally and necessarily determined.

> *The individual as the product of deterministic historical and economic forces leaves serious art with nothing but stereotype and ideology, all dead rhetoric. The individual remains the only source of imaginative recreation of society...We need to see self as a potential ground for renewal and not as something stale and socially made.*[20]

However, freedom and the capacity to change do not arise through the workings of a solipsistic and determined rationality, but through the seductive duel/dual relation with the irreducibly Other. Rationalists may object that the world of seduction is unpredictable, hazardous and irresponsible. Seduction would reply that this is substantially the case but that the 'security' which reason claims to offer is a delusion (in itself dangerous) which nevertheless exacts a high price in terms of desiccation and banality.

I have suggested that the processes of Seduction are generalised throughout Barker's work. This is not to argue seduction is somehow the 'essence' of Barker or indeed that seduction is being recommended as some sort of alternative ideology. My point is that our responses to drama — as to the rest of life — are never purely empirical; we bring to it a host of preconceptions and expectations which determine our 'reading'. I have suggested that authoritative 'rationalist' discourses influence these preconceptions to a degree of which we not always fully aware. Further. that there are effective processes which I have generally designated under the name of Seduction the operations of which 'rational' discourse marginalises or represses in the interests of maintaining the closure of its own structures. The affective impulse behind this movement locates itself in the appetite for reassurance which develops with mass interdependency. The seductive processes, however, are experienced as intrinsically 'dramatic' because in any such encounter, the sense of challenge, the sense of a vast opening–up of possibilities, energises the participants.

Barker has persistently referred to his theatre as 'a theatre of catastrophe'.[21] Most of his plays are set in catastrophic circumstances either immediately before or immediately after fairly massive social breakdowns. As I have already suggested, this enables him to detach his characters from the normalising structures of social and economic interdependency thereby opening up the range of possible behaviours. Catastrophe, however, according to Baudrillard, goes much further than this : it abolishes causality:

> *It submerges cause beneath the effect. It hurls causal connections into the abyss, restoring for things their pure appearance or disappearance (as in the apparition of the purely social and its simultaneous disappearance in panic). This is not, however, a matter of chance or indeterminacy; rather it is a kind of spontaneous connection of appearances, or of the spontaneous escalation of wills, as in the challenge.*[22]

Alternatively, in the world of causality there is no catastrophe but only crisis. Similarly, the idea of chance belongs essentially to rationality. The concept presumes that no other form of connection apart from causality can exist; it is equivalent to the 'accidental'. This is a way of dismissing the wider significance of an event: accidents can happen to anyone. In the world of seduction, however, there are no accidents and there is no chance: everything is destiny. This is what, in the rational world, gives the accident its peculiar seductive charm.

Direct Seduction of the Audience

In some of his more recent work, Barker has 'set the tone' by addressing the audience directly in a prologue. The earliest example of this style of direct address is the dramatic monologue *Don't Exaggerate* where a dead soldier talks to the living ; this is not an exegesis, nor a narration (though it contains elements of both) but a torrent of fluctuating and alternating emotional impulses which appear to interact with the audience's impassivity. This interaction — active performer/passive audience — is, in fact, quite often mirrored within the frame of Barker's drama where a highly vocal character confronts another character who remains silent (e.g. Stucley and Ann in Scene 1 of *The Castle* — see Chapter 4). In the prologues to *The Last Supper* and *The Bite of the Night*, the intention to seduce is obvious and, in the latter case, quite explicit:

> *I charm you*
> *Like the Viennese professor in the desert*
> *Of America*
> *My smile is a crack of pain*
> *Like the exiled pianist in the tart's embrace*
> *My worn fingers reach for your place*
> *Efficiently*[23]

In his first stage play, *Cheek*, Barker presents the audience with a working class youth whose main asset is a talent for seductive utterance and the title of the piece indicates this. In the prologues, Barker deploys a variety manoeuvres to 'engage' the listener. In the example cited above, seductive strategy is reflected in the 'use' of weakness (pain).

I bring you an invitation
Oh, no, she says, not an invitation
Yes
We are all so afraid
Yes
An invitation to hang up the
Suffocating overcoat of communication
Hang it up[24]

Here, the prologue comically interjects objections to his speech on behalf of an apprehensive audience — the second and fourth lines (the second line, in particular, is reminiscent of the comedian, Frankie Howerd). The prologue persists, however, with mock severity ('Yes…Yes…'). The bold type in the seventh line signals a forceful delivery which is softened by a more cajoling tone in the following line; this manoeuvre frequently occurs in *Don't Exaggerate* and the prologue to *The Bite of the Night*: the speaker gets carried away into a display of excessive rage or becomes stentorian, whereupon, realising this is untoward, he attempts to mollify with a more wheedling tone. A process of persistently abolishing his own performance.

The next statement is immediately followed by an example of another ingratiating tactic:

And those with biros write upon your wrist
The play contains no information
Aren't you tired of journalists?
Oh, aren't you tired of journalists?[25]

Sometimes Barker attempts to establish a conspiratorial relation with his audience but the repeated question here, the tone of which parodies the blatant, gossipy populism of its target, seeks to draw listener and speaker into a mutual empathy. This particular prologue ends with the speaker breaking off in mock horror:

When the poem became easy it also become poor
When art became mechanized it became an addiction
I lecture!
Oh, I lecture you! (A terrible storm of laughter)
Forgive!
Forgive![26]

The laughter here is, of course, the 'canned' laughter of much popular entertainment and its use is ironic. The ending of the prologue, nevertheless, demonstrates a final undercutting of the speaker's own performance which involves a renunciation of authoritarian communication — lecturing.

Through all the pantomime, however, Barker makes it possible for the actor to induce a complicity.

The essential seductive mode of these prologues is the challenge:

> *Should we not*
> **I know it's impossible but you still try**
> *Not reach down beyond the known for once*[27]

As he implies later in the same prologue, Barker views much contemporary drama as the theatrical equivalent of pre–cooked, pre–digested food; everything must be instantly meaningful:

> **Clarity**
> **Meaning**
> **Logic**
> **And Consistency**
> *None of it*
> *None*
> *I honour you too much*
> *To paste you with what you already know…*[28]

As I indicated above the seductive relation is a mutual one — subject/Other rather than subject/object. The use of the word 'honour' here indicates the respect for radical alterity which this form of engagement implies. Seduction is the alternative to the manipulative, controlling relation which characterises communication in our society and it is with this in view that one must consider Barker's frequent denunciations of 'authoritarianism' both in the theatre and society at large.[29] This rejection does not merely concern the crude manipulations of the commercial stage but, perhaps more particularly, the Brechtian aim of presenting an analysis of 'the world' along the theoretical lines of — let us say — 'The Street Scene'.[30] For Barker such approaches invariably entail the degradation of language itself:

> *If language is restored to the actor he ruptures the imaginative blockade of the culture. If he speaks banality he piles up servitude.*[31]

The importance of speech is also highlighted by Levinas in somewhat similar terms:

> *Speech is a relationship between freedoms which neither limit nor negate, but affirm one another.*[32]

Seduction within the Action of the Plays

This is ubiquitous, continuous and often quite explicit, forming through various different permutations a central dramatic facus. More often than not, the action of seduction is indirect — we seduce the one in order to seduce the other; in this way, character A's seduction of character B can indirectly seduce the audience. This is, in fact, by far the most common situation in drama: it is the actor's strategy. Barker's very first stage play, *Cheek* (1970), focusses on an idle and cynical working class youth's attempts to fulfil his sexual ambitions through his rhetorical skills (hence the title). 'Cheek' — defined in the Concise Oxford Dictionary as 'effrontery' or 'shameless audacity' — is calculated to challenge without alienating the other to the extent that they simply break off the encounter; the tactic of refusing shame is often deployed by Barker's characters. In essence it challenges by transgressing the limits of the (socially defined) self and attempting to lure the other into a complicity, a pact. Laurie's schemes end in failure because, like all effective seducers, he is seduced himself — to a considerable extent by his own articulacy.

In *Claw* (1975) and *Stripwell* (1975), speech seductions or attempted speech seductions in particularly extreme circumstances comprise the crucial dramatic episodes of the plays. These attempts at an extreme reversal all have in common the aim of deflecting or diverting another from their established truth, — from their identity. The same is the case in *Fair Slaughter* (1977), where the central figure, Old Gocher, is incarcerated in a prison hospital; seventy–five years of age, he has been transferred from an old people's home where he murdered a fellow inmate on account of a dispute which originated in their mutually antipathetic political loyalties; Gocher is a dedicated communist. The action turns around his success in persuading one of the warders, Leary, to help him to escape. The rigidly ideological Biledew in *Claw* is clearly the theatrical prototype of Old Gocher whose biography is traced through a series of flashbacks beginning in Siberia 1920 where he made his first contact with Communism via the Franco–British Expeditionary Force. Young Gocher's initial insight into the nature of capitalism occurs when the allies' entire military machine grinds to a halt because their 'capitalist oil' has frozen. His life–long commitment to Communism is forged when he shares a prison cell with Trotsky's engine driver. This man, known only as Tovarish (comrade), is killed by the Whites and Gocher is given the task of burying the body of his new–found friend in the frozen Arctic ground. As a symbol of his commitment, he severs the Russian's hand and retains it.

The 'present' of the play begins with Old Gocher attempting to conceal the bottled hand from his gaoler, Leary, whom he subsequently persuades to assist him to escape in order to return the hand to the buried body of its rightful owner in Russia. Other flashbacks present Gocher's struggle to maintain his ideological commitment and survive in England from the twenties through the Second World War to the present. He sacrifices personal success as a popular entertainer; his wife leaves him because he puts Russia before her and his relationship with his only child is poisoned owing to his bitterness in the face of consistent political failure. Gocher is typical of a number of Barker characters who commit themselves to a truth — in this case the truth of communism. His posture puts him in the position of having habitually to resist seduction in order to maintain this ideal in the alien environment of England.

Throughout the play Gocher's antagonist is the capitalist Stavely — his C.O. in Russia and his theatrical manager; later he appears as the owner of a distillery. Leary helps Gocher to escape and, through a delicately portrayed and highly comical process of sustained mutual deception, the pair arrive on the steppe — actually the South Downs — and prepare to lay the hand to rest. At this point the geriatric Stavely appears, having wandered off an old folks outing; he is subjected to an impromtu trial and found guilty by the now throughly anti–capitalist Leary. Gocher, however, feels sorry for the old man and intervenes to save him just before dying himself haloed in a beatific vision of Tovarish in glory. Leary runs off with the hand and Stavely is left alive squalidly gloating over a crumpled reproduction Picasso.

Once a seduction is embarked upon what rules and moral obligations then operate on the participants? Leary, the gaoler, initially transgresses by offering to turn a blind eye to Gocher's escape. This gesture in turn obligates Gocher to persist with the escape — a course of action he had by this time, in his heart, probably relinquished with a degree of relief. He escalates the challenge for Leary by asking him to come with him and help him return the hand. Leary does and the two become engaged in what is clearly a mad relation with the Brighton train becoming the Trans–Europe Express and the South Downs the Siberian Steppes. This would no doubt be pure farce were it not for the fact that Gocher is dying (in itself one of the most powerful seductions). Leary initiates the illusion to satisfy the old man but it becomes clear that Gocher is aware of this: in part he feels he owes it to Leary — who has just sacrificed everything — to persist. All the same, he continues to exploit the situation and to challenge:

> GOCHER: *Don't give in to patriotism, Leary. It's their way of closing yer eyes… (LEARY looks at him. Long pause) You are sitting on the Trans-Europ Express, and I don't think you know why. You have done an action out of impulse, and it's frightened you. (Pause) Pity's not enough. You've got to find an ideology.*
> *(They look at one another. LEARY suddenly points out of the window.)*

LEARY: Look! It's the USSR!
GOCHER: We never stopped in Poland! What happened to Poland?
LEARY: No one wanted to get off.
GOCHER: (grabbing the bottled hand) Tovarish! Your homeland!
LEARY: Congratulations, Tov!
GOCHER: His long exile, over!
LEARY: (breathing deeply) Soviet air!
GOCHER: Arise, ye starvlings from your slum-bers, Arise, ye crim-i-nals of want!
(He breaks down into a fit of deep coughing. LEARY watches, helplessly. Pause GOCHER recovers.) We'll have trouble finding him. (LEARY looks appalled). A skeleton with one hand missing. Won't be easy. (Pause) Will it? Not easy.[33]

The fundamental rule is not to break off the seductive duel which either party can do by invoking the reality principle: this would be a betrayal provided the momentum of challenge and counter-challenge does not slacken. Leary cunningly evades an ideological lecture, resisting Gocher's 'legacy', by announcing the USSR; Gocher temporarily nonplussed recovers to pick up the challenge and join in the triumph, using the momentum of this, to launch his next challenge — finding the corpse. Another typical feature of seduction very much in evidence here is bluff. Both participants know, and know that the other knows they know, but they can't acknowledge this and know that the other can't acknowledge etc. Here Barker's stage directions are essential — the pauses, the looking at each other at crucial moments. It has often been said of Barker's writing that everything is articulated — there is no subtext. Arguably, this could be true of the passage just cited — in that nothing of substance is **communicated**. Alternatively, this is a very pregnant 'nothing', an intense and spiralling complicity.

Eventually, as the hand is about to be interred, a geriatric Staveley, Gocher's capitalist oppressor, wanders on. Leary insists on an impromptu trial and makes an impassioned speech for the prosecution. As with Claw, and Stripwell, this is the speech of his life and he indicts Staveley, the capitalist, as ultimately guilty of all that he has suffered as a gaoler. When he demands immediate execution, much to his disgust, Gocher, who has already murdered one geriatric without compunction, pleads for mercy. As a result of the seduction, a reversal has occurred with the gaoler becoming the hardline ideologist and the dying man a 'sentimental' humanist. Leary now insists that the hand is rightfully his:

GOCHER: Give me Tov.
LEARY: No.
GOCHER: Give it to me.
LEARY: You are not fit to have Tov.

> GOCHER: *Christ, do not lose sight of your humanity! You have so much good in you!*
> LEARY: *To be licked up by that specimen. To be sucked on by his class.*
> GOCHER: *Keep an open heart, son. Feed your heart. The angrier you feel, the more you have to feed the heart!*
> LEARY: *I do what Tov says!*
> GOCHER: *Fuck him! He was an ordinary bloke, that's all. Think for yourself. They stuck Lenin under glass, and look what they have done in his name.*[34]

One could say that Gocher's return of the hand allows him to bury his ideological commitment and release his humanity. But the hinge of his apostasy here, however, is that he does not want to bequeath to Leary the sterile life that he himself has led. As he dies in a heavenly vision of Tovarish in glory (who appears armed with dahlias), it is his 'disciple', Leary, who goes off with the hand.

In the figure of Toplis in *Crimes in Hot Countries*, Barker explores a character almost directly antithetical to Gocher. Though both, in the context of capitalist society, are subversive revolutionaries their personalities function in entirely different ways. Gocher's ambition is to achieve an historical status in the context of a Marxist/Leninist ideology, a truth; Toplis, based on the historical Toplis, ringleader of the First World War Etaples Mutiny, is dedicated purely to the business of seduction. Since escaping the death penalty as a mutineer by seducing his guards, he has lived by seducing women. At the beginning of the play he returns to the military life at a desert outpost of the post-war British Empire. Appropriately disguised as a conjuror, he sets about repeating his previous triumph amongst the bored and disaffected soldiers. Eventually, the mutiny breaks out in a bizarre auction scene where Toplis' rhetoric involves him in an increasingly irrational duel with T. E. Pain — Barker's version of Lawrence of Arabia. Toplis' subversion, however, is entirely irresponsible and amoral with no thought to the consequences of his actions. His personal lifestyle is predicated upon temporary imposture and moving on before chickens come home to roost. When Erica, the governor's daughter, who has fallen in love with him, commits herself by shooting his would-be executioners, he refuses or is unable to respond to the gesture. Concerning his revolutionary activities, he admits:

> TOPLIS: *I have to conjure with them, Erica. Like the women on the boulevard. See what I can drive them to. In their madness, I taste something like life…*[35]

As Baudrillard states:

> *To challenge or seduce is always to drive the other mad, but in a mutual vertigo: madness from the vertiginous absence that unites them, and from their mutual involvement.*[36]

Toplis' lack of truth and consequent lack of reality is parallelled in the play by continual references to his death and implications that he is a ghost.

In his more recent plays, Barker has demonstrated an increasingly sophisticated and complex awareness of the processes and interactions of seduction. A common scenario is the 'magisterial' relation — 'teacher' and 'pupil', a classic example of a duel where the participants attempt to drive each other mad. In *Fair Slaughter*, Old Gocher's relation to the warder, Leary, is essentially 'educative'. In *That Good Between Us*, the transformation of the degraded police informer, McPhee, is effected by Major Cadbury who functions largely as a guru. In *Crimes in Hot Countries*, the subversive, Toplis, supplants Pain as the soldiers' intellectual mentor. In *The Bite of the Night*, the pedagogic relation of Professor Savage and his student, Hogbin, figures prominently. Perhaps the most spectacular deployment of this relation is in *The Last Supper*: based on the Christian archetype, it extends the ritual leavetaking from 'disciples' by a guru into ritual murder and anthropophagy. The prophet, Lvov, maintains a seductive relation with each of a very diverse group of 'apostles': he secures their permanent adherence by persuading them to kill him and eat his corpse. What Barker does show, before the denouement, is that each relationship is a vertiginous and unrelenting duel between master and disciple, so that Lvov's final gesture of invoking his own death seems the only escalatory response available to him which is extravagant enough to cope with them all: as Lvov knows full well, his grisly condition, that the Lvovites consume his corpse, is utterly binding according to the unspoken, unwritten 'law' of their seductive engagement. This is what Baudrillard is referring to when he talks of 'an unremitting obligation to respond and outdo'.[37] In doing this, Lvov seduces them beyond the transcendental law, beyond the prohibition, and this, of course, becomes 'the secret' which binds them and will be the source of their power. It is therefore appropriate that the act of cannibalism should not be seen by the audience and the fact that it is literally 'unspeakable' is emphasised in the final scene:

> SUSANNAH: *He had the flavour of —*
> ALL: **Don't mention it!**
> SUSANNAH: *He had the texture of —*
> ALL: **Don't dare describe it!** (*Pause. The knot of disciples drifts, first one way, then another. The cloud passes overhead.*)[38]

These are the final lines of the play. There is clearly a convergence here with Baudrillard's discussion of the secret reversibility at the heart of imperium:

> *Thus the pope, the grand inquisitor, and the great Jesuits or theologians all knew that God did not exist; this was their secret and their strength.*[39]

It is also a common practice amongst clandestine social groups who regard themselves as élites to have their members undergo ritual humiliation in order the better to bind them together with unspeakable secrets: the individual concerned is compelled to traduce the boundaries of their identity. In *The Loud Boy's Life*, Barker illustrates this in Act 1 Scene 4, where the 'loud boy', Ezra Fricker is attending a dinner of the Ancient Order of Savages; when the scene begins, he has just been coerced, much to his embarrassment, into performing an impromptu strip-tease.

In the world of reason, motivation is founded always in positive causality and individual behaviour is structured upon biological drives modified according to various social and psychological determinants. In the world of seduction, purely negative forces are capable of intervening decisively like pools of accumulated anti-matter. The secret is a negative force. So is the meaningless. In *The Bite of the Night*, one of the principal characters, Gay, persistently attempts to impose an intellectual order upon her chaotic life; this order is forcibly maintained in the face of seduction and violence by an authoritarian exclusion of the other:

> GAY: *You say yes as if I were supposed to feel bereft. You say yes with a hush, as if you know something that I do not —*
> CREUSA: *I don't know either —*
> GAY: **I am tired of this idea there's something else. It's used to bully me, to hit me on the brow and brain and crush my life —**
> CREUSA: *I don't know either, I said —*
> GAY: *There's nothing else!*[40]

Seduction in its most common sexual context is frequently encountered in Barker's plays. *The Bite of the Night* is structured around the archetypal seducer, Helen of Troy. Barker's adaptation of *Women Beware Women*, focusses directly on the power of a sexual relationship to transform those involved; similar relationships are featured strongly in *Victory* (Bradshaw and Ball), *Crimes in Hot Countries* (Toplis and Erica), *The Power of the Dog* (Sorge and Ilona). In the latter case, a complicity is established between the two characters which relates to the mysterious death of Hannela, Sorge's ex-mistress and Ilona's sister. Such transformations do not necessarily 'improve' the individuals concerned.

The Power of the Dog, subtitled *Moments in History and Anti-history*, explores further the truth/seduction antithesis. Barker sees historical narratives as ideological constructions which seek to assimilate and annex the individual. A classic example is Marxism-Leninsim, in this play embodied in the character of Stalin who believes that he has 'emptied the cupboard' of his own individuality in order to achieve a total identification with his ideology. As such, he exhibits the kind of insanity which generally attends upon absolute power. The anti-history scenes focus on a Hungarian photographer/model, Ilona, who has collaborated freely with both Nazis and Allies in order to pursue her career across the battlefields of Europe. She represents an antithesis to Stalin in that her strategy is founded upon her seductive charm:

> ILONA: … *Shall I tell you what I believe? I believe that every murder is an acquiescence, and every victim possessed the means of her escape. I believe in your eyes and in your mouth you own the means of your salvation, whether you want to be loved, or whether you want to be saved. At the door of the restaurant, or the gate of the camp*[41]

The charmed life she leads is also contingent upon accepting everything and resisting nothing:

> *To anyone who thinks it is a mystery, how we cope with so much history. I say the answer lies in pain, what my mother went though I can again. Swallow the monster and don't strain, murders from the Bosphorus to the Hebrides render all complaints absurdities. Don't ask what makes the system, if it is a system, work, cover your indignation with your foot, don't think that black stuff is burned bodies, really it is only soot…*[42]

As her words here suggest, Ilona refuses the order of truth/reality by bluffing herself as well as other people. As he becomes conscious of his approaching death, Stalin finds himself increasingly charmed by the notion of the accidental:

> STALIN: *I would give up all the authority I possess to meet a beautiful woman on a train…*
> *It is a sad fact I cannot meet a woman on a train unless both the woman and the train are commandeered for me. But of course that entirely removes the significance of the occasion. Accident, which is the essence of experience, has been eliminated from my life…*[43]

Because he is concerned to bequeath to posterity a true likeness of himself, he orders a photographer to be randomly selected from 'somewhere in the Polish desert'. This engineers the final scene of the play — captioned 'History Encounters its Antithesis' — where Ilona and Stalin meet, providing the former with her most extreme challenge and the latter — possibly — with his 'woman on the train.'

I have already referred to the functioning of the secret in *The Last Supper*. In *Not Him*, the final play of *The Possibilities*, secrets are even more important. A woman greets her husband who returns after seven years of warfare brandishing a bag of severed heads. Both husband and wife have changed, however, and she is undecided whether the man who arrives really is her husband. Initially she counters this uncertainty by making herself an enigma for the man — she wears a veil. The piece ends after she has made love and killed him. It is clear that the third character in the play — the wife's female companion — shares with her a secret complicity the substance of which is witheld from the audience. When the friend states, after the killing, — 'You have killed your husband...', she is promptly hushed by the wife; as with the eating of Lvov, the event is unspeakable. The killing itself occurs offstage and is only communicated to the audience in an indirect and cryptic fashion:

> SECOND WOMAN: And did he yell?
> WOMAN: He cried out with the awful cry of disbelief that all men make, and his eyes were searching for their focus.[44]

In the first place, the woman's response is ambiguous: she could be referring to sexual climax here: it is only the Second Woman's following line that makes the audience re-interpret these words. Further, her use of the words 'all men' — suggests she may have killed others. Earlier, under pressure from the 'husband', her female companion had attempted to deny that soldiers had passed through the village. When he objected that he had seen wheeltracks, the story was amended and he was informed that his 'wife' had hidden — 'Even from her allies'. The women have quite clearly had to deal with the prospect and possibly the actuality of the rape and murder that the 'husband' boasts of inflicting on the enemy. What happened then is their secret; we are aware of its presence and its power.

The salient feature of the piece is the sustaining throughout of the ambiguity concerning the man's identity — 'Him?' or 'Not him?' The 'wife' has two possibilties: the man is her husband with all the burden of moral and social implications that implies. Alternatively, he is merely 'another' raping and murdering soldier whom it is possible to enjoy sexually then kill without compunction. Her neighbour appears prepared to collude with whatever choice she makes and, in fact, actively assists in keeping options open. This is rendered possible because his long absence and the war have clearly changed the man so that he confronts his wife with a different identity. In the world of reason and logic, one of the fundamental axioms is that it is not possible for something simultaneously both to be the case and not be the case; this is sometimes referred to as the law of non-contradiction. Seduction abolishes this:

> Seduction does not consist of a simple appearance, nor a pure absence, but the eclipse of a presence. Its sole strategy is to be-there/not-there, and thereby produce a sort of flickering, a hypnotic mechanism that crystallizes attention outside all concern with meaning. Absence here seduces presence.[45]

In *Not Him*, the man is both 'him' and 'not him'; objectively, the issue is never resolved and the piece is all about this paradox. The woman's desire thrives on the ambiguity, — as she states in the final lines:

> WOMAN: Shh… (*Pause. She sits.*) He thrilled me. Oh, his words of violence, how he thrilled me! And his murders, how they flooded me with desire…
> SECOND WOMAN: It was him…
> WOMAN: It was him. Did he think I was fooled?[46]

As in a number of these plays, the ending presents us with a final twist: having murdered, the woman discovers that she can not merely accept but positively relish the idea that she killed her husband. Her final sentence indicates the potential for reversal in the seductive duel. For the audience, there is a contradiction between the two sentences — 'It was him. Did he think I was fooled.' The man asserts consistently that he is the husband, so how is he attempting to 'fool'? Possibly by appearing as 'other', by assuming the swaggering and boastful identity of the military butcher in order to render himself sexually attractive. (His exaggerated claims and the heads business seem to be a performance calculated to impress.) The woman, however, appears to be ready to fool herself: in the absence of objective proof, she will believe what she wants to believe. Baudrillard's dictum applies to them both:

> To seduce is to die as reality and reconstitute oneself as illusion. It is to be taken in by one's own illusion and move in an enchanted world.[47]

The line also suggests that she sees the man as concealing his identity and attempting to deceive her in order to escape his destiny — seduction is destiny. Such a perspective renders him ethically inferior and serves to justify her action. Now that the event has passed, she imposes its 'truth'.

In *The Bite of the Night*, the student Hogbin is about to be killed by the thuggish soldiers Epsom and Gummery; like Claw and Stripwell, he talks for his life — as it happens, — with some success. He suggests to them that their lives are unfulfilled:

> EPSOM: You 'ave the echoing tones of an advert for a mother's tonic —
> HOGBIN: **Well, yes, because great truth shares language with great error**, and luscious sunsets are reflected in slum windows… (*Pause. HOGBIN waits.*)
> GUMMERY: (*At last*). Yes…[48]

For Gummery, this is no mere deflection from an immediate task; Hogbin has shattered the basis of his whole life. He undergoes a complete transformation, akin to religious conversion, and from what he says later it is clear that he has been seduced, not by rational argument, but essentially by the metaphor Hogbin in his extremity employs here. This brings us to language.

Seduction of Language

The ambiguity of this heading is apposite. Language is obviously the medium of Barker's drama but, though it is perceived as being deployed by the characters, it posseses a peculiar force of its own and often actively resists the attempts of individuals to control it. Language, as is suggested in the example cited above, seduces in its own right. In *The Europeans*, set in the aftermath of the siege of Vienna by the Turks in 1683, Katrin struggles to describe the experience of being raped to a priest charged with the duty of recording Turkish atrocities:

> *… then one of them threw up my skirt — excuse me —*
> *(She drinks)*
> *Or several of them, from now on I talk of them as plural, as many headed, as many-legged and a mass of mouths and of course I had no drawers, to be precise —*
> *I owned a pair but for special occasions. This was indeed special but on rising in the morning I was not aware of it, and I thought many things, but first I thought — no, I exaggerate, I claim to know the order of my thoughts WHAT A PREPOSTEROUS CLAIM — strike that out, no, among the cascade of impressions — that's better — that's accurate — cascade of impressions — came the idea at least I DID NOT HAVE TO KISS.*
> *(Pause)*
> *The lips being holy, the lips being sacred, the orifice from which I uttered my most perfect and religious thoughts only the grass would smear them but no.*
> *(Pause)*
> *Can you keep up? Sometimes I find a flow and then the words go — torrent — cascade — cascade again, I used that word just now I have discovered it, I shall use it, probably ad nauseam, cascading! But you —*
> *(Pause)*
> *And then they turned me over like a side of beef, the way the butcher flings the carcass, not without a certain familiarity, coarse-handling but with the very vaguest element of warmth, oh, no, the words are going, that isn't what I meant at all, precision is so — precision slips even as you reach for it, goes out of grasp and I was flung over and this MANY MOUTHED THING —*
> *(She shudders as if taken by a fit, emitting an appalling cry and sending the water flying. The nun supports her. She recovers.)*[49]

This speech exemplifies one of the most striking features of Barker's dramaturgy — namely his ability to forge text which reflects sensitively the fluctuations of a consciousness struggling to cope in extremity. Katrin's discourse appears to strive for objectivity — for accuracy and truth — against the insidious seductions of language. It is arguable, however, that even her apparent successes are in fact seductions and the reason why the word 'cascade' recommends itself does not lie in its precision but in its ameliorative connotations and its capacity to anaesthetise — albeit only a little — one aspect of an unbearable trauma. Katrin comments later that she feels she is mad and, certainly, the structure of her discourse here is by no means 'rational' with its narrative impulse constantly baffled, deflected and seduced. In order to convey this, Barker ruptures the 'normal' patterns of syntactical relations; sentences begin forcefully, then break off without explanation; on other occasions they flow on, one into another, without any punctuation but, above all, speech persistently doubles back to comment on itself. One is aware of different levels of consciousness — consciousness of the rape itself, of language and of the silent other who is transcribing all this; in particular, what kind of complicity exists between Katrin and the latter who, because he is invisible, in darkness, merges and is in turn complicit with the audience? Baudrillard characterises the action of seduction as a kind of 'flickering'; in this case what flickers is Katrin's sense of identity — constantly dissolving itself then re-emerging elsewhere.

This same fluctuation characterises the prologues discussed above — as well as much of Barker's published poems (e.g. *Don't Exaggerate*). It is comparable particularly with the celebrated prose style of the French novelist, Louis Ferdinand Céline. In her analysis of Céline's style, Julie Kristeva isolates two typical features:

> ... *segmentation of the sentence, characteristic of the first novels; and the more or less recuperable syntactical ellipses which appear in the late novels.*
> *The peculiar segmentation of the Célinian phrase, which is considered colloquial, is a cutting up of the syntactic unit by the projected or rejected displacement of one of its components.*[50]

Kristeva argues that the ejected element is desyntacticised but is typically charged with the speaker's emotion and moral judgement — an exclamation, an interjection, exaggeration or abuse. Hence the logic of this 'message' dominates the logic of syntax. Kristeva goes on —

> *This 'binary shape' in Céline's first novels has been interpreted as an indication of his uncertainty about self-narration in front of the Other. Awareness of the Other's existence would be what determines the phenomena of recall and excessive clarity, which then produces segmentation. In this type of sentence, then, the speaking subject would occupy two places: that of his own identity (when he goes straight to the information, to the rheme) and that of objective expression, for the Other (when he goes back, recalls, clarifies).*[51]

As in Barker's prologue to *The Last Supper*. Céline often pre-empts the Other's response to his narration in the narration itself. This is facilitated by the de-syntacticising process further developed in the later novels through the use of the famous three dots. This is Céline's prologue to his final novel. *North*:

> *Sure, I tell myself, it'll all be over soon... whew!... we have seen enough... at sixty-five and then some what difference can the worst H... Z... or Y superbomb make... they're zephyrs!... nothings! the only terrible thing is this feeling of having wasted all my time and all those myriatons of effort for that hideous satanic horde of alcoholic cocksucking flunkeys... lady, lady! have pity!... 'Shut up and sell your gripes!'... hell, why not?... I'm willing but to whom?*[52]

Obviously, this technique allows the fluctuating emotion of utterance to dominate the demands for clarity and objectivity made by syntax. Kristeva also points out that this stylistic device allows for long syntactic periods in which the sense of each phrase overflows into the totality; it is rhythmic, reflecting easily current levels of intensity; it refuses the normal subordinations and hierarchical structures of syntax; it allows the invasion of non-meaning and the dominance of intonation.

Kristeva sums up the style thus:

> *It is as if Céline's stylistic adventure were an aspect of the eternal return to a place which escapes naming and which can be named only if one plays on the whole register of language (syntax, but also message, intonation, etc.) This locus of emotion, of instinctual drive, of non-semanticised hatred, resistent to logico-syntactic naming, appears in Céline's work, as in other great literary texts, as a locus of the ab-ject. The abject, not yet object, is anterior to the distinction between subject and object in normative language. But the abject is also the non-objectality of the archaic mother, the locus of needs, of attraction and repulsion, from which an object of forbidden desire arises. And finally, the abject can be understood in the sense of the horrible and fascinating abomination which is connoted in all cultures by the feminine or, more indirectly, by every partial object which is related to the state of abjection (in the sense of the non-separation subject/object). It becomes what culture, the sacred must purge, separate and banish so that it may establish itself as such in the universal logic of catharsis.*[53]

I have quoted this passage in full because it seems to me that Kristeva is describing here — within the terms of a feminist-psychological discourse — a locus very similar to Baudrillard's seductive and Levinas's ethical relation — a relation beyond the subject/object polarities where the identity of self and other is indefinite before the ego has erected its narcissistic structures of dominance and repression. Apart from the stylistic connection with Barker's writing, there are two other areas of convergence which come to mind here. Firstly, there is the pre-emptive gesture which Barker describes thus:

> *... the character gives a performance that he then proceeds to subvert. So that they pre-empt other characters' right to judge them. The character says — 'I know myself, — my qualities. So don't think you can accuse me because I already know that.' That's the way a lot of political figures negotiate.*

> *You see the performance attempt and the failure. And the reason the performances are put up is because people need carapaces in order to endure what history has imposed upon them within the play. The girl in THE EUROPEANS who's been raped, plays complete absorption and a complete understanding of her situation. She continually plays self-knowledge but as the play progresses this is continually demolished.*[54]

This insistent movement towards completeness and self-possession is what Kristeva is alluding to in the quotation above from 'Psychoanalysis and the Polis' when she asserts culture's need to purge itself — to resist the abject. For Derrida it manifests the desire of the subject for self-presence, for origin, for an end to differance, for truth. It is a gesture of exclusion and exclusivity aimed at 'The Other'.

Abjection

Excretion, in particular, is 'partial object... related to the state of abjection'. Partial, in respect of Freud's anal phase, as representing a crucial arena of ego-mastery in the constitution of the 'subject' proper. As Derrida relates in his essay on Artaud, 'La Parole Soufflée':

> *Proper is the name of the subject close to himself — who is what he is — and abject the name of the object, the work that has deviated from me. I have a proper name when I am proper. The child does not appropriate his true name in Western society — initially in school — is not well named until he is proper, clean, toilet-trained.*[55]

One of Barker's most scatological works is *The Hang of the Gaol*. Set in the ruins of a burnt out gaol, the action comprises the progress of an official enquiry into the cause of the fire. In our society, the convicted criminal represents the abject par excellence. Like the insane, the convict does not possess the requisite degree of 'self-control' to be permitted the normal 'freedoms'. Abjection is forced upon him — most notably, as Barker astutely indicates, in the routine of 'slopping out':

> *STAGG: No. You called them —*
> *JANE: Bucket-shitters (Pause. He stares) I thought everybody called them that.*
> *STAGG: No.*
> *JANE: Well, they do shit in buckets, don't they?*[56]

For Jane, wife of the governor, Cooper, the prisoners' group identity is defined by this process — the essential element of which is that the individual is not permitted to dispose privately of his personal waste. In the opening scene of the play two prison officers contemplate the ruin:

> *UDY: The old screws never left a gaol without depositing a turd in it.*
> *WHIP: Burglar's trick.*
> *UDY: Superstition, obviously. One I adhere to. Sort of symbolic clearing out. Shedding of guilt. (He looks round quickly.) Anybody coming?*
> *WHIP: I don't think I will.*
> *UDY: (Removing his coat and jacket) Help you, Michael. Face the enquiry with an open mind...[57]*

Udy then proceeds to deposit his ritual turd on stage; Whip makes the attempt but without success. Superstition apart, by sharing the ritual with Whip, Udy is attempting to set the seal on a complicity which will bind them together in the face of the enquiry. The central focus, however, of the play and the nexus of the scatological thematic lies in the character of Jardine, the civil servant who conducts the official inquiry. This role is one of the most theatrically impressive and subtley-drawn of the entire corpus of seventies' drama. I will limit myself here, however, to the description of Jardine proffered by his colleague, Matheson:

> *MATHESON: ... Mr Jardine wants you to take the piss out of it. Do you follow? Shit all over the job. And yet persist in doing it. It's a sort of grand machismo.*
> *JARDINE: Careful, Elizabeth.*
> *MATHESON: He is one of these people psychiatrists describe as partially complete. Only by abusing what he's doing can he extract the slightest satisfaction from it. Like a man who can't enter a woman unless he's poured vitriolic filth all over her. Called her a prostitute and so on.*
> *JARDINE: Elizabeth, you are being very stupid.*
> *MATHESON: He is a first-class civil servant but he will wallow in this self-contempt...[56]*

Matheson's comment is cut short by Jardine physically attacking her, — a response which would tend to confirm her analysis. In fact, Jardine's sole source of pride lies in his incorruptible and remorseless professional integrity. As such, he provides an outstanding example of a character in which the sanctity/profanity opposition alluded to by Kristeva with its accompanying cathartic rituals is particularly strong. The denouement of the play comes when the Labour Home Secretary, Stagg, requires Jardine to falsify the enquiry's findings for 'political considerations' — to help Labour win the coming election. Jardine, reluctant to forgo his knighthood, gives his assent at the Coopers' leaving party:

> *STAGG: ... George, where does a bloke go for a slash round here?*
> *JARDINE: Where ye're standing, I imagine. Down the leg.*
> *STAGG: Join me, will yer? Piss for socialism. Piddle Martyrs we shall be. (JARDINE goes to him, stands at his shoulder. They urinate.) Well, son? What's it to be?*
> *JANE: He is urinating on my Harry Wheatcrofts...*
> *JARDINE: I am laying down my honour. For your honour.[59]*

The combination of Jardine's moral collapse with this striking physical gesture is remarkably significant; it is an expression of contempt, a form of abuse directed at the Coopers and the social class the Coopers represent but it is also conscious self-degradation, a disburdening of guilt (as Udy suggested), a ritual of complicity, a defiant flaunting of the state of abjection — which is ultimately the badge of their subservience. It is the gesture that reduces Jardine to the same level as the Labour Home Secretary, as the prison officers, Udy and Whip, — as the 'bucket-shitters'. Because the carceral he has just 'got the hang of' is England. As Matheson remarks in her final line:

> MATHESON: *England brings you down at last...*[60]

There are numerous other examples of Barker's interest in the state of abjection; in *The Bite of the Night*, there is the public 'marriage-bed rite' of Savage and his wife Creusa; in *The Europeans*, there is Katrin's insistent publicising of her rape which culminates in the public exhibition of her childbirth. Through being taken in by their own illusion, fooling others in order to fool themselves, Barker's characters regularly refuse conventional shame thereby reversing the normal interpersonal dyamics of the situation. This is particularly the case in the play I wish to consider next.

3

JUDITH — A SEDUCTION

Judith, published in 1990, is based on the apocryphal story of the eponymous Jewish heroine who conveyed herself secretly to the tent of Holofernes, her country's oppressor, seduced and then murdered him, taking away as trophy the decapitated head of her victim. Besides the two central protagonists, Barker includes another woman who accompanies Judith referred to in the dramatis personae as 'the Servant'; such is the function initially ascribed to this character by Judith when the two women arrive at Holofernes' tent but Barker also describes her as 'An Ideologist' — something which becomes more apparent later in the play. In *The Possibilities*, Barker dealt with the aftermath of this episode in a play entitled *The Unforeseen Consequences of a Patriotic Act* where Judith, having lost the power of speech, has retired to the country to give birth to the murdered Holofernes' child. When a representative of the state comes to urge her back into public life, Judith describes her action as 'a crime' because murderer and victim had desired each other. When the representative extends her hand to Judith to reassure her, the latter cuts it off with the words:

> *I cut the loving gesture! I hack the trusted gesture! I betray! I betray!*[1]

Barker is focussing again upon the point where personal morality, the intuitive sense of the ethical, is violated in the interests of the political. Where the face to face with the other (*That Good Between Us*), in which Levinas locates the foundation of the ethical, is savagely betrayed.

    Judith begins with Holofernes alone in his tent. As emerges in subsequent dialogue, he has completed his plan of battle; with this and his own charismatic presence in the ranks, he is complacent that he will defeat Israel, as he has done before, and put the entire nation to slavery and the sword: the conclusion is foregone. The moment of the play, then, lies in a strange hiatus between action and event — all the more strange because the event is a slaughter. This is the familiar Barker territory of the catastrophic — a twilight zone where the 'real', regulated world of social ties and obligations fades and desire is free to express itself.

Holofernes begins with what appears to be a solioquy reflecting on death. The status of the speech — as soliloquy — is undermined when the general interjects an order to others outside his tent to enter. This introduces immediately an area of ambiguity: conventionally audiences trust the soliloquy, assuming that the absence of any other characters onstage disposes of any motive for pretense on the part of the speaker. This is a device Barker uses in other dramas to play upon the ambiguities of the performer/role split. (There is a similiar situation in *The Europeans*, Act I Scene 3, which begins with what appears to be a soliloquy from Katrin but auditors emerge from the darkness.) In spite of seeming to be absorbed in his own thoughts, Holofernes is acutely aware — more so than the audience — of what goes on round about him. His words indicate a considerable level of intellectual sophistication:

> *For while victory is the object of the battle, death is its subject, and the melancholy of the soldiers is the peculiar silence of a profound love.*[2]

Holofernes presents himself as being aware of of his own seduction here; victory is the rational justification for battle, its object, but it is not why he desires battle. As I suggested, in seduction, the end is seen as a means to a means. This same melancholy love is celebrated in the works of the Great War poets, the rational, socialised object of whose poems is, in complete contradiction, the 'pity' and the condemnation of war. The fact that Holofernes' self–analysis is not befogged by humanistic ideology is clear when he talks of his 'cruelty'.

> *But cruelty is collaboration in chaos, of which the soldiers are merely the agents. (p. 49.)*

His words show a self–conscious awareness of his posture as challenging conventional morality which he mocks:

> *Because I walk among the dead they will ascribe to me feelings of shame or compassion. This is not the case. Rather, I am overcome with wonder. I am trembling with a terrible infatuation… And some generals talk of necessity. They talk of limited objectives. There are no limitations, nor is there necessity. There is only infatuation.(p. 49.)*

When the two women enter, they kneel silently; Judith uncorks a bottle. Holofernes remarks disparagingly that he does not drink and there is a long pause. When the servant appears to offer Judith to the general, her register, in contrast to his, is colloquial, comonplace and obviously ingratiating:

> *I heard — futile now, I see — I heard — you liked women. (p. 49.)*

Holofernes announces that he wishes only to talk of death. The servant's response — that Judith is similarly pre–occupied with mortality — appears an ingratiating lie and her persistence prompts Holofernes to seize and choke her. Up to this point, Judith has remained silent — leading Holofernes to dismiss her as 'shallow', 'a bitch', 'a thing that giggles'. She lacks any quality of 'otherness' — a vacuous sexual object which has been proffered many times before, the Same. He focusses upon the servant as being responsible for their intrusion. When Judith utters her first line —

> *You are killing my property. (p. 50.)*

he is startled and engaged. He realises that he has been mistaken concerning the relative status of the women, that he is, in Judith's eyes, dignifying a mere object, a slave, with an interest which should be beneath him. He is also intrigued at the manner of her intervention — not humanitarian — which suggests that she may be as 'cruel' as himself. This latter aspect may have been a successful bluff on her part. Her objection to his behaviour is, anyway, a challenge to his authority to do as he pleases — and she herself begins to take on the status of a challenge. After a pause, he attempts to reassert his status with the put–down:

> *I do not wish to fuck tonight. (p. 50.)*

A little later, he makes the admission:

> *I do like women, but for all the wrong reasons. And as for them they rapidly see through me. They see I only hide in them, which is not love. They see I shelter in their flesh. Which is not love. Now, go away. (p. 50.)*

As is made clear later, nothing that any of the parties to this dialogue says may be taken entirely at face value. Expressions like this, which may appear to be an admission of weakness, can in fact be a tactic to enlist sympathy or a challenge.

A pause is broken by the cry of a sentry and Holofernes commences the next section of dialogue by suddenly appearing to question his whole career:

> *HOLOFERNES: It is of great importance that the enemy is defeated.*
> *JUDITH: Oh, yes!*
> *HOLOFERNES: Or is it? Perhaps it only seems so.*
> *JUDITH: Seems so?*
> *HOLOFERNES: Always the night before the soldiers die I think — perhaps this is not important after all. Perhaps it would be better if the enemy defeated us. I mean, from a*

universal point of view. Perhaps my own view is too narrow.
JUDITH: (Thoughtfully) Yes... (p. 50.)

This, in itself, is a very seductive gesture because of its openness; it seems to invite participation on an equal level and Holofernes appears effectively to be putting his very identity— as war hero — into play. Judith's measured and cautious response, leads on to Holofernes dismissing serious consideration of the idea and escalating the duel by rapping out another challenge —

Take your clothes off now. (p. 51.)

He interjects this order almost as an aside in the middle of a speech. I do not think this is so much a calculated tactic as a drop onto a different level of consciousness. He makes clear some lines later exactly what her attraction is:

I long to be married, but to a cruel women. And as I lay dying of sickness in a room, I would
want her to ignore me. I would want her to laugh in the kitchen with a lover as my mouth
grew dry. I would want her to count my money as I choked. (p. 51.)

This seems to represent a denial/refusal of any possiblity of love and one would think that the invitation he seems to give here would be quite satisfactory for Judith's purpose — a purpose well–known to the audience. She finds, however, in spite of a massive effort of will that she is unable to comply with his instruction. In her confusion, she turns on and attempts to dismiss the servant whom Holofernes, now triumphant, detains — probably to increase Judith's embarrassment.

There is another pause, after which, Holofernes sums up; he seems to interpret her confusion as meaning that she came not merely with the idea of fornication, but of loving him.

I am a man who never could be loved. I am a man no woman could find pitiful. Pity is love.
Pity is passion. The rest is clamour. The rest is just imperative...
When a woman loves a man, it is not his manliness she loves, however much she craves it. It is
the pity he enables her to feel, by showing, through the slightest aperture, his loneliness. No
matter what his brass, no matter what his savage, it creeps, like blood under a door...(p. 53.)

This again could be perceived as a kind of challenge. If one is seduced by weakness and vulnerability, then the apparent humiliation he forces on Judith can rebound upon the perpetrator: Holofernes puts himself in danger of pitying her. There is a reversal and weakness becomes strength. Perhaps Holofernes realises this and when Judith expresses the desire to dress, he escalates the encounter by removing some of his clothes — exposing himself. Judith's request for confirmation of his bloody intentions for the following day is perhaps an attempt to confirm her own murderous purpose. Her increasing impatience with the servant's interventions shows that she resents this third party view of the duel. She confesses her own unhappiness to him and there is an important silence:

> *(Long pause. They look at one another.)*
> HOLOFERNES: *I can't be loved (p. 55.)*

The reiteration of this point suggests again that the possibility or the hope is very much in his mind. Something flows between them in the look.

Holofernes returns to philosophising by contending that the sole purpose of existence is reproduction, that this is absurd, and in view of this, his career as a military butcher is no less moral than any other. Judith suggests an alternative:

> *Yes, but if life is so very — is so utterly — fatuous, should we not comfort one another? Or is that silly? (p. 55.)*

At this point the servant, obviously feeling that things are drifting the wrong way, intervenes to cut short this almost tender melancholy and, indirectly, to bring Judith back to her original objective:

> *Tomorrow you'll be different! You'll have done the killing of a lifetime! Tomorrow you won't know yourself! 'Did I go on about death?'*
> *'Was I miserable?' Off with yer skirt, darling! (p. 56.)*

Judith responds to this:

> JUDITH: *All right, let's fuck. (p. 56.)*

She tries to dismiss the emotional validity of their previous intensity, to undercut the enchantment of seduction:

> *You want me to say how much I, how magnificently you, all right, I will do, I'm far from educated, so I'll stop pretending, and anyway, nothing you say is original, either. Do I insult you? Do I abolish your performance? It needs abolishing. (Pause. The servant turns away in despair. HOLOFERNES stares at her, without emotion. The pressure in JUDITH dissipates. She shrugs.) I am reckoned to be the most beautiful woman in the district. So I thought I had a chance. (She goes to pick her clothing off the floor. She stops and lets out a scream. The scream ceases. She remains still.) (p. 56.)*

Judith tries to force an objective view on their encounter — not only of Holofernes who is not 'original', but also of herself — 'reckoned to be the most beautiful woman'. The servant clearly thinks Judith has gone too far in insulting Holofernes but the latter controls any impulse of anger he feels and allows her to exhaust her tension. When he resumes, he does so from where he left off with a challenging admission:

> HOLOFERNES: *And yet I want to be. (Pause) I, the impossible to love, require love. Often, I am made aware of this. (Pause) (p. 56.)*

When the servant, seeing an opportunity of salvaging the situation, encourages him to continue with this, he silences her:

> HOLOFERNES: *Do you think I can't see you? (The SERVANT is transfixed.) Your mask. Your fog. Do you think I can't see you? (Pause) (p. 56.)*

The moment is highly ambiguous. What does Holofernes mean? The Servant is 'transfixed' presumably at the possibility that Holofernes 'sees through her' — i.e. knows why she is pandering to him. Is he bluffing? or is he merely objecting to her patently false interest in him? What he says immediately after this, although it appears to be — and may actually be — generalisation, takes on a very particular significance: he is referring initially to his need to be loved:

> *The way in which it asserts itself is as follows. Frequently I expose myself to the greatest danger. I court my own extinction. Whilst I am exhilarated by the conflict I am also possessed of the most perfect lucidity. So absolute am I in consciousness, yet also so removed from any fear of death, I am at these moments probably a god. (p. 56.)*

Is Holofernes suggesting that he knows the women have come to kill him, that in his godlike 'lucidity' he has perceived their intention, that he is deliberately courting death? Whatever may be the case on his part, his words must surely make this impression, however fleeting, on the women? When the women arrived, they came concealing a secret; Holofernes sensed this and he is now attempting to turn the seductive power of their secret against them, while maintaining his enigma for them. To return to Baudrillard:

> *…I know the other's secret but do not reveal it, and he knows I know it but does not let it be acknowledged: the intensity between the two is simply the secret of the secret… Only at the cost of remaining unspoken does it maintain its power, just as seduction functions from never being spoken or desired…*[3]

Holofernes, however, goes on to say that after the ecstasy of courting death, he is haunted by the need to know that, if he had indeed died, some other person would have died of grief for him:

> *I am not the definition of another's life. That is my absent trophy. I think we live only in the howl of others. The howl is love. (Pause) (p. 57.)*

This is the reverse of the desire he expressed earlier for a 'cruel women'. The Servant, again trying to use the opportunity to put matters back on course, gives Holofernes a 'lecture' to the effect that 'strong' men must show a woman a little weakness — as a kind of concession to their inferior dignity. In response to this Holofernes shows a complete collapse — he bursts into tears and clasps the Servant. The tears may be 'real' but it would seem likely, especially in the light of what has just been said, that Holofernes is deploying them tactically. In fact the violence and immediacy of his response suggest he may be mocking the Servant — particularly as the stage directions state that he should release her just as abruptly as he he seized her. The effect of this could be quite comic though there should be no overt hint of a comic intention on Holofernes' part, He then proceeds to tell them what a weak and cowardly child he was:

> *There was none weaker than me. (p. 57.)*

His confession of abject weakness leads on to a description of how he learned to compensate for this:

> *But being weak I discovered cunning. I learned to say one thing, knowing it would satisfy the expectation, whilst carrying on a second and more secret conversation with myself. I led people away from my true intention, my speech became a maze, I used speech to trap my enemies, my speech was a pit, I lived in speech, making it a weapon. (p. 57.)*

Judith, however, draws the immediately relevant conclusion from all this:

> *You mean, nothing you say is true? (He looks at her.) I don't mind that. I am perfectly able to lie myself. I am almost certainly lying now in fact. (p. 57.)*

Surprisingly, perhaps, Judith says she finds this a great relief:

> *Excellent! Forgive my hysteria, it was the pressure, the sheer suffocating pressure of sincerity. And now I am light! I am ventilated! A clean dry wind whirls through my brain! I intend to kill you, how is that for a lie? And that must mean I love you! Or doesn't it! Anything is possible! I think now we have abandoned the search for truth, really, we can love each other! (p. 58.)*

Judith's exhilaration is owing to a number of factors: a) she is courting death in the manner Holofernes claimed he did ('I intend to kill you') — perfectly lucid and 'godlike'; b) she has freed herself of the burden of her original intention — her duty, (she may or may not kill Holofernes); c) she is energised by the opening up of possibilities ('Anything is possible') which is characteristic of seduction.

> *The relief of knowing you are simply an element in a fiction! I think before this moment I never was equipped to love. (p. 58.)*

Judith has put her own identity into play — Jewess, widow, mother of about–to–be–massacred children — the magnitude of the stakes in this seductive game adds to its intensity. As I indicated in the relevant chapter, seduction relieves one of all obligations one is under in respect of the Law. In Barker's earlier treatment of this subject in *The Unforseen Consequences of a Political Act* (one of *The Possibilities*), Judith says of this moment:

> *I could not have cared if he dripped with my father's blood, or had my babies' brains around his boot, or waded through all Israel.*[4]

The moment of seduction detaches the individual from both personal and political history.

Interestingly, it is not Holofernes' confession of social inadequacy that engages her (if love is pity) but his admission that he lies:

> *When you told me you could not help yourself lying I fell in love with you. That was the moment. (p. 58.)*

She ends by encouraging Holofernes to continue lying, thereby maintaining a seductive world of pure artifice. The point is, however, not merely to lie — which would be to tell the truth by saying the opposite — but to preserve the dangerous tension of ambiguity:

> JUDITH:…*Lie, do lie! (Pause)*
> HOLOFERNES: *I know why you're here. (Pause. The SERVANT stares.)*
> JUDITH: *I know why I came.*
> HOLOFERNES: *I know what you intend.*
> JUDITH: *I know what I intended.*
> HOLOFERNES: *I know it all.*
> JUDITH: *I knew it all. (Pause) I knew it all. And now I know nothing.*
> *(He looks into her.)*
> HOLOFERNES: *We love, then.*
> JUDITH: *Yes.*
> HOLOFERNES: *And I, who is unlovable, I am loved*
> JUDITH: *My dear, yes… (Pause) (p. 58.)*

Judith's immediate response to Holofernes' challenge is quite inspired. While preserving the secret as secret, she acknowledges his challenge in the most direct way but implies that, although she may have come with a particular intention, Holofernes has caused her to abandon it — very flattering to his sense of himself as godlike. Their professions of love are particularly interesting with regard to the 'lying' pact. Baudrillard states:

Only signs without referents, empty, senseless, absurd and elliptical signs absorb us.[5]

And:

Seduction lies with the annulment of the signs, of their meaning, with their pure appearance.[6]

Both parties here have agreed that what they say is strictly 'meaningless' — which serves to intensify their duel. So when Holofernes says 'We love, then' and Judith affirms it, the words are not a communication, — they are the thing itself, pure presence.

While they embrace, the Servant intervenes — almost like a chorus. She presents the perspective of 'reality', the world of truth, concerned not with processes but ends, not with the magic of superficial appearances but interpretation:

> *One of them is lying. Or both of them. This baffles me, because whilst Judith is clever, so is he…*
> *How brilliant she is! How ecstatic she is! She convinces me! But she must be careful, for with lying, sometimes, the idea, though faked, can discover an appeal, and then we're fucked! (p. 58–59.)*

In the charmed world of seduction, language ceases to be instrumental: we can be seduced by our own words.

When Holofernes appears to be asleep in Judith's arms, the 'servant' changes:

> *SERVANT: (abandoning her persona) Judith… (p. 60.)*

From this point on, she drops her role of procuress or servant and addresses Judith as an equal. Realising that Judith has been seduced, she puts as much pressure on her as she can to carry out the murder:

> *SERVANT: Israel commands you. Israel which birthed you. Which nourished you. Israel insists. And your child sleeps. Her last sleep if–*
> *JUDITH:* **I am well drilled.** *(She glares at the SERVANT. The SENTRY cries. Pause. Judith goes to the sword.)*
> *SERVANT: Excellent. (She unsheaths it.)*
> > *Excellent.*
> > *My masterful.*
> > *My supreme in.*

> *My most terrible.*
> *My half–divine. (JUDITH raises the weapon over Holofernes)*
> HOLOFERNES: *(without moving) I'm not asleep. I'm only pretending. (Pause. The sword stays.)*
> *My dear.*
> *My loved one.*
> *I'm not asleep. I'm only pretending. (Pause. JUDITH closes her eyes.) (p. 60.)*

It becomes clear here why Barker added the description of 'ideologist' to the Servant in the dramatis personae. The echoing of the servant's formal, ritual invocations by Holofernes serves to underline the conflict here between power on the one hand ('My masterful', 'My terrible') and desire on the other ('My dear', 'My loved one.') The surprise, however, is Holofernes' final seductive gesture: he puts his life absolutely in Judith's hands: he has reversed their situations:

> HOLOFERNES: *I can win battles. The winning of battles is, if anything, facile to me, but.*
> JUDITH: *My arm aches!*
> HOLOFERNES: *But you.*
> JUDITH: *Aches!*
> HOLOFERNES: *Love.*
> JUDITH: *My arm aches and I lied!*
> HOLOFERNES: *Of course you lied, and I lied also.*
> JUDITH: *We both lied, so —*
> HOLOFERNES: *But in the lies we. Through the lies we. Underneath the lies we.*
> SERVANT: **Oh, the barbaric and inferior vile inhuman bestial and bloodsoaked monster of depravity!** *(p. 60–61.)*

It is interesting that Barker writes Holofernes' last speech here with a single full stop at the end of each sentence rather than a short line of dots which would have indicated an intention to complete the sentence. These are complete because Holofernes is alluding to an unspoken pact which must not be uttered but which is pointed at in 'we'. His words, coupled with the gesture of complete vulnerability, paralyse Judith. She repeats the Servant's slogan but cannot act:

> JUDITH: **Oh, the barbaric and inferior** — *(Seeing JUDITH is stuck between slogan and action, the SERVANT swiftly resorts to a stratagem, and leaning over Holofernes, enrages JUDITH with a lie.)*
> SERVANT: *He is smiling! He is smiling! (With a cry, JUDITH brings down the sword.) (p. 61.)*

The notion that Holofernes is grinning in confident anticipation of another easy victory is enough momentarily to abolish his performance in Judith's eyes; the very intensity of their pact is turned against itself and she has ample power to kill him.

The Servant rushes to complete the job of removing Holofernes' head; she is practical and businesslike but Judith is stunned. Her speech indicates two violently dislocated levels:

> *A right bitch cunt, I was, nearly ballocked it, eh, nearly — (She staggers.)* **Oh, my darling**
> **how I** *— (She recovers.) Nearly poxed the job, the silly fucker I can be sometimes, a daft bitch*
> *and a cunt brained fuck arse — (She staggers.)* **Oh, my — Oh, my —** *(p. 61–62.)*

This parallels the levels of mind and brute body into which the servant has hacked Holofernes. A constant theme in Barker's work is the struggle between the state and the individual for possession of the individual's agony, their suffering. In this case, the Servant's seizure of the head forms part of this expropriation:

> *We take the head because the head rewards the people. The people are entitled symbolically to*
> *show contempt for their oppressor. Obviously the spectacle has barbaric undertones but we.*
> *The concentration of emotion in the single object we etcetera. So. (p. 62.)*

Barker here is clearly satirising the double standards of the state 'ideologist' — condemning but endorsing 'barbarism' for its own purposes.

Judith, focusses upon the headless body and announces her intention of making love to it. I have already indicated that, in the world of seduction, death does not end the engagement; in fact, *The Last Supper* shows how it can be used to prolong it indefinitely. The Servant is utterly horrified and protests:

> *SERVANT: It demeans your triumph and humiliates our —*
> *JUDITH: How can he be an enemy? His head is off.*
> *SERVANT:* **Enemy. Vile enemy.**
> *JUDITH: You keep saying that...! But now the head is gone I can make him mine, surely?*
> *The evil's gone, the evil's in the bag and I can love! Look, I claim him! Lover, lover, respond to*
> *my adoring glance, it's not too late, is it? We could have a child, we could, come, come, adored*
> *one, it is only politics kept us apart!*
> *SERVANT: I think I am going to be sick...*
> *JUDITH: No, no, count to a hundred...*
> *SERVANT: I will be made insane by this!*
> *JUDITH: You weren't insane before. Is it love makes you insane? Hatred you deal admirably*
> *with. Come, loved one...! (She lies over Holofernes's body. The SERVANT is transfixed with*
> *horror.) (p. 62.)*

Judith's comment here is significant: we are presented with two contrasted atrocities — first the killing and severing of the head, then the attempted necrophilia. The first is applauded by the state as an act of heroism, the second abhorred — not least because this behaviour is hardly consistent with a heroine — which is what the state will now require Judith to be.

After the failure of Judith's attempt to love Holofernes, she is physically unable to move. This hysterical paralysis reflects her own mental state — she cannot adjust to what has happened. Dramatically this is convenient because it poses the problem in a very acute way; they have to escape, but the Servant will have to persuade Judith to come to terms with her action before they can do this. First she says she will find Judith a husband and prophecies a vision of idyllic marital bliss and contentment. This is probably totally counterproductive: in the light of what has just taken place, such a dream can never attain any degree of reality for Judith. Thereafter, when Judith says that she wants to go but cannot, the Servant asserts that she is being punished by God for trying to make love to Holofernes. Judith asks the Servant to pray for her — she does but to no avail. As the Servant is leaving, Judith gives 'a profound cry of despair' which causes her companion to stop. The Servant suddenly has an idea:

> *I say god. I mean Judith. (Pause) I say Him. But I mean you. (Pause. The cry of the SENTRY is heard. The SERVANT places the head on the ground, and comes back to JUDITH. She kneels before her, and leaning on her knuckles, puts her forehead to the ground. Pause. JUDITH watches.)*
> *JUDITH: You are worshipping me. (p.64–65.)*

It is no doubt the extremity of the moment which lends the Servant the persuasive power of her next speech which articulates a number of recurring Barker themes and deserves to be quoted in full:

> *SERVANT: Firstly, remember we create ourselves. We do not come made. If we came made, how facile life would be, worm-like, crustacean, invertebrate. Facile and futile. Neither love nor murder would be possible. Secondly, whilst shame was given us to balance will, shame is not a wall. It is not a wall, Judith, but a sheet rather, threadbare and stained. It only appears a wall to those who won't come near it. Come near it and you see how thin it is, you could part it with your fingers. Thirdly, it is a facility of the common human, to recognise no act is reprehensible but only the circumstances make it so, for the reprehensible attaches to the unnecessary, but with the necessary, the same act bears the nature of obligation, honour and esteem. These are the mysteries which govern the weak, but in the strong are staircases to the stars. I kneel to you. I kneel to the Judith who parts the threadbare fabric with her will. Get up, now. (Pause, JUDITH cannot move. The SERVANT counts the seconds. She perseveres.) Judith, who are those we worship? What is it they possess? The ones we wrap in glass and queue half-fainting for a glimpse? The ones whose works are quoted and endorsed? The little red books and the little green books, Judith, who are they? Never the kind, for the kind are terrorized by grief. Get up now, Judith. (Nothing happens. Pause) No, they are the specially human who drained the act of meaning and filled it again from sources fresher and —*

(JUDITH climbs swiftly to her feet.) (p. 65.)

The entire argument, from the Servant's point of view, is pure hypothesis; as she herself said earlier:

... you can know a thing and still not know it. (p. 56.)

Her words, however, are sufficient to transform Judith from a state of complete and abject powerlessness to one of godlike dominance. Again, this demonstrates the action of the reversal process in seduction: by refusing the overwhelming burden of grief and shame, these negative emotions become instead a positive glorying in her action. She must escalate the stakes. Judith experiences again the sense of liberation she experienced when she felt free to lie to Holofernes: she will use the murder to create a powerful new self. She has taken over the absolute character Holofernes displayed at the beginning of the play. The first person she tests her shamelessness on, ironically, is the Servant whom she humiliates by treating like a slave:

JUDITH: **Who said you could get up**. *(The SERVANT stops.) And any version that I tell, endorse it. For that'll be the truth. (p. 65.)*

She abolishes any kind of truth apart from that which she herself creates; her word is all the reality there is. It is only by escalating the game in this way that Judith can be re-energised through the opening of new possibilities:

I shall be unbearable, intolerably vile, inflicting my opinions on the young, I shall be the bane of Israel, spouting, spewing, a nine-foot tongue of ignorance will slobber out of my mouth and drench the populace with the saliva of my prejudice, they will wade through my opinions, they will wring my accents out of their clothes, but they will tolerate it, for am I not their mother? (p. 66.)

Barker has been criticised for a writing which, as fantasy, has no purchase on the 'real' world, yet I have no difficulty in recognising the 'power-crazed' mentality Judith demonstrates here. While humiliating the Servant by forcing her to cut her hair off, Judith reflects on testing further her superhuman status:

To kill your enemies, how easy that is. To murder the offending, how oddly stale. Real ecstasy must come of liquidating innocence, to punish in the absence of offence... (p. 66.)

Because of her role as ideologist, Judith particularly despises the Servant, who is temporarily discomforted with her companion's new-found character but on the whole approves:

> *...for you nothing is really pain at all.*
> *Not torture. Death. Or.*
> *Nothing is.*
> *It's drained, and mulched, and used to nourish further hate, as dead men's skulls are ground*
> *for feeding fields... (p. 67.)*

Sewage disposal is a persistent Barker metaphor for the ideological/political scene; because pain and suffering is continually justified, expropriated, used by political ideology, it is also, and in consequence, not experienced fully by the individual. Although the Servant thinks that Judith has been safely secured for the state — which will tolerate her tyranny and corruption — Judith's last words before she leaves the stage:

> *Israel*
> *Is*
> *My*
> *Body! (p. 67.)*

suggest another reversal. Israel claims Judith, but she claims Israel, a transformation similar to the case of Stalin in *The Power of the Dog*.

If one were to consider this play from the Stanislavskian point of view of a structure of consistent objectives, it is clear that this could be appropriate only for the Servant, the ideologist, who maintains throughout the play the superobjective of killing Holofernes and maximising the political capital therefrom. In a way, this is an important part of her function — to offset the seductive relation between the other two. It could be objected that I have advanced an interpretation of the play, a practice which I have, on the whole, tended to condemn. I would argue that, given a text, it is the job of those staging it to take the written lines and turn them into actions — mainly speech-acts; in considering Barker's text I have been concerned to describe what is **happening**. My approach has been ontological and subjective, not ideological and objective. I believe that the 'thought' expressed in the text of *Judith* (as well as in Barker's other writings) points strongly to the kind of focus which I have attempted to outline in this study.

4

THE CASTLE

Perhaps the most highly acclaimed of Barker's plays to date has been *The Castle* which was first performed as part of the 'Barker season' in the RSC Pit at the Barbican in 1985. At that time, the drama was widely perceived as being principally concerned with the Reaganite intensification of the arms race and with 'Greenham Common' style feminist oppositional values; this connection, while not without substance, does not dominate the play and certainly does not sanction the extrapolation of simple political or social 'messages'. The text comprises one of the richest and most densely written of Barker's entire oeuvre, providing an intellectual canvas surpassing in its breadth while simultaneously depending upon a symbolic weave of astonishing economy and tight integration. In this final chapter, I wish to examine this major work in some depth, an exercise which will entail an examination of literary/symbolic elements as well dramatic considerations since both are relevant to the theoretical concepts of seduction I have advanced.

The plot is relatively straightforward. An English knight, Stucley, returns home to his domain after years spent fighting in the Crusades. His followers have been killed or fallen by the wayside; only a single retainer the appropriately named Batter and a captive Arab engineer, Krak, accompany him. However, while he has been away, the women have evolved a different lifestyle which is feminist, collective and non-exploitative of human or natural powers. Further, Stucley's wife is involved in this on the level of a personal as well political commitment insofar as she is the lesbian lover of Skinner, a ploughman's widow, whose feminism is both militant and profoundly ideological. Stucley is disgusted by what appears to him to be rank negligence of his estate but his chief concern is to find Ann and to resume a relationship which infatuates him and which he has carried like a grail in his heart through all his military travails. She informs him that she has been unfaithful and that he should leave. In a blind fury, he sets about 'restoring order' and implements the construction of a massive castle designed by Krak. The latter, hating his captors, an alien cut off from any positive emotional ties with the land in which he is held, intends the castle

as an engine of destruction aimed as much at its possessors as their potential
foes. Stucley also reestablishes his lapsed priest, Nailer, as bishop of his own
unique sect of Christianity — the church of Christ the Lover. Against this
array of male power — spiritual and temporal, the opposition of the women
can do little. Skinner, the most resolutely opposed to the castle, realising that
Ann's love for her is ebbing away, in desperation seduces and murders the
builder — Holiday. She is tortured in the dungeons of the castle, tried for the
murder and sentenced by Stucley to be turned loose with the rotting corpse
of her victim chained to her. As Stucley becomes increasingly paranoid
ordering more and more fortifications and corresponding increments in his
police state, Ann seduces Krak whose awakened emotions introduce
confusion into his hitherto singleminded devotion to the castle. Ann,
pregnant with his child, pleads with Krak to run away: he tells her that
there is nowhere to go — the castle is inescapable. She kills herself along
with her unborn infant and the action is followed by an epidemic of suicides
amongst pregnant women who throw themselves off the castle walls. The
grief-stricken and by now quite mad Stucley is given the coup de grace by
his bailiff, Batter, who in consultation with Nailer asks Skinner to become
head of a feminist-type earth-mother religion. Skinner, transformed by her
sufferings, has remained at the castle and has become the focus of a secret
and quasi-religious popular veneration. When she refuses to prop up Batter's
state, he offers power directly to her. In a surge of desire she promises
vengeance on all who have made her suffer but almost immediately realises
that she will be 'too cruel' and declines the offer. Krak steps out of the
shadow of the castle wall and insists she accepts: the play ends with Skinner
struggling to recall a time when 'there was no government' as jets streak
overhead.

Considered from the perspective of the basic interrelations of the
characters, a clear pattern emerges which focusses on Ann who seduces or
has seduced the other main roles. She is worshipped by her husband, Stucley,
whose subsequent degeneration can be seen as a consequence of her
rejection. If anything, she is even more essential to Skinner's moral universe.

> SKINNER: ...*They talk of a love-life, don't they? Do you know the phrase 'love-life', as if
> somehow this thing ran under or beside, as if you stepped from one life to the other, banality
> to love, love to banality, no, love is in the cooking and the washing and the milking, no matter
> what, the colour of the love stains everything, I say so anyway, being admittedly of a
> most peculiar disposition I WOULD RATHER YOU WERE DEAD THAN TOOK A STEP
> OR SHUFFLE BACK FROM ME....*[1]

Skinner herself makes clear later in the action that she is shattered not by the
return of male power or even by her torture but by the loss of Ann's love.

After Skinner, Ann seduces Krak, similarly rocking his cosmos to its very foundations. Her suicide precedes and precipitates the final catastrophe — the mass suicide of the pregnant women. Stucley's assassination, and the offer of power to Skinner. All three of her 'victims' commit themselves to various 'truths' — they resist. Ann steadfastly refuses to sacrifice any of her instinctive desires in the interests of ideology or even of sparing others pain. Her power to seduce others lies in her own openness to seduction.

Stucley is, as I have indicated committed to truths: he has been engaged in an ideological conflict, the Crusade, and his agonisings over religious matters show that his theological concern is not mere hypocrisy:

> I found the church bunged up with cow and bird dung, the place we married in, really, what — (pause) So I prayed in the nettles. (p. 8.)

His 'faith' has been reinforced insofar as he has suffered for it. Returning home to his wife, he extends his religious feeling to her:

> ... I have seen your face on tent roofs... (p. 7.)
> I was saying to the Arab every hundred yards I have this little paradise... (p. 8.)
> ...I who jumped in every pond of murder kept this one thing pure in my head, pictured you half-naked on an English night... (p. 8.)

This kind of exaggerated veneration of woman, within the predominantly medieval context of the play, strongly accords with the chivalric 'courtly love' phenomenon, the secular counterpart of the cult of the Virgin Mary. Stucley himself has struggled to remain 'pure'. When Cant, one of the women, proffers sexual intercourse, he reacts violently and is immediately ashamed:

> CANT: My man's not come back so you do his business for him — here — (She goes to lift her skirts. STUCLEY knocks her aside with a staggering blow)
> STUCLEY: I won't be fouled by you, mad bitch, what's happened here, what! I slash your artery for you! (He draws a knife) Down you, in the muck and nettle! (She screams) MY TERRITORY! (He straddles her)
> BATTER: HEY! (STUCLEY wounds her, she screams)
> STUCLEY: My shame, you — LOOK WHAT YOU'VE MADE ME DO! I've — I've (He tosses the knife away, wipes his hand) To come home and hear vile stuff of that sort is — when I am so clean for my lover is — no homecoming, is it? (p. 4.)

Stucley's violence is directly occasioned by the need to defend his 'purity': he is aroused but simultaneously threatened by Cant's desire. As such, he experiences a momentary loss of self-control which results in the mutilated/mutilating act of wounding Cant's breast — an act of which he is immediately ashamed. It is the first act of violence in the play and provokes

1. The homecoming of the Crusaders. *The Castle*, Act I, Scene 1.

wide resonance. It signals an important and ubiquitous theme in the drama — the archetypal equating of the land and the female body: Stucley emphasises this with his cry — *'My territory!'* — as he straddles Cant on the ground. A few lines later in the scene, Ann says — *'A woman, this country...'* (*p. 5.*) Stucley's rage at this particular point is because his 'territory' has 'returned to nature' — the result, not of sloth, but of the deliberate policy of the women; as Skinner states later in the scene:

> SKINNER: *First there was the bailiff, and we broke the bailiff. And then there was God, and we broke God. And lastly there was cock, and we broke that, too. Freed the ground, freed religion, freed the body. And went up this hill, standing together naked like the old female pack, growing to eat and not to market, friends to cattle who we milked but never slaughtered, joining the strips and dancing in the commons, the three days labour that we gave to priests gave instead to the hungry, turned the tithe barn into a hospital and FOUND CUNT BEAUTIFUL that we had hidden and suffered shame for, its lovely shapelessness, its colour all miraculous, what they had made dirty or worshipped out of ignorance... (p. 6.)*

Here again this female freedom is linked to the hill where the scene is set (Ann tells Krak to get off her hill). The hill, in fact, becomes the focus of the struggle which develops between male and female forces. Stucley who has concentrated all his energies on resisting seduction, resisting change, preserving his ideal, has vested everything in control and the violence of brute mastery. His action in wounding Cant prefigures his 'wounding' of the hill through the building of the castle; Skinner, conversely, later exerts her witchcraft to activate the natural power of the hill against this imposition:

> SKINNER: *OLD HILL SAYS NO......ROCK WEEPS AND STONE PROTESTS...* (p. 15.)

It is left to Krak, however, hitherto practically silent, to step into the confusion of Stucley's encounter with Cant and restore order:

> KRAK: *So much emotion, I think, is perfectly comprehensible, given the exertion of travelling, and all your exaggerated hopes. Some anti-climax is only to be expected.*
> STUCLEY: *Yes. (He shrugs) Yes.*
> KRAK: *The only requirement is the restoration of a little order, the rudiments of organisation established, and so on. The garden is a little overgrown, and minds gone wild through lack of discipline. Chaos is only apparent in my experience, like gravel shaken in water abhors the turbulence, and soon asserts itself in perfect order. (p. 4.)*

Krak demonstrates here that he is a rationalist, espousing the scientific perspective of a universe ordered by inexorable laws. The apparent chaos of appearance belies the 'true' underlying reality whose principle is founded upon the highly classical notion of equilibrium — balance, economy, equivalence. Though Stucley embraces Krak — at one point literally — as architect of his castle, he does not embrace the Arab's rationalism; his own universe remains inexorably fatal and — in spite of his attempts at resistance — seductive.

Stucley, temporarily restored to spirits and all childish enthusiasm, chases off to find his wife:

> STUCLEY: ...I run to my wife's bedroom. Catch her unprepared and all confusion. Oh, my lord, etcetera, half her plaits undone! Oh, my lord and all... (p. 5.)

However, no sooner does he leave the stage than his wife appears. She has apparently been watching them and has emerged to confront Krak:

> ANN: My belly's a fist. Went clench on seeing you, went rock. And womb a tumour. All my soft rigid. What are you doing on my hill?
> KRAK: (Turning) Looking. In so far as the mist permits.
> ANN: It always rains like this for strangers. Drapes itself in a fine drench, not liking to be spied on. A woman, this country.... (p. 6.)

In an interview in *New Theatre Quarterly* 8, Barker said:

> ...actually no conclusions can be arrived at by expertise, only by instinct. I think that one of the great powers of Greenham, although it has been ignored, and is probably destroyed now. But as a terribly important historic metaphor, it does stand for the power of instinct — which is what the play The Castle is about.[3]

Ann's immediate hostile reaction to Krak is entirely instinctive and totally irrational. When Skinner appears moments later, she reinforces Ann's feeling and acts instantly to 'stab him'. Both women sense that they may have lost their only chance of averting catastrophe:

> ANN: I hope that wasn't — I do hope that wasn't — THE MOMENT AFTER WHICH — the fulcrum of disaster — I hope not.
> SKINNER: Miss one moment, twice as hard next time. Miss the next time, ten times as hard the next.
> ANN: All right — (p. 5.)

As the play unfolds, their instinct is proved correct. Another element of Krak's 'Reason' evident in the quotation above is the gaze: when asked what he is doing, he replies simply — 'Looking.' The stage directions at the head of the scene, the beginning of the play, commence with —

> A Hill. A MAN, wrapped against the rain, stares into a valley... (p. 3.)

He continues to 'stare' until, a full page later, he is asked the object of his gaze by Stucley:

> KRAK: I am looking at this hill, which is an arc of pure limestone. (p. 4.)

This is clearly a gaze of some considerable intensity and, combined with Krak's enigmatic taciturnity, represents a significant element in the interactive dynamics of the scene. Later when Stucley is presented with the results of Krak's deliberations — the plan for the castle — the moment is echoed by the theatrical text in a very spectacular fashion:

> STUCLEY's long stare is interrupted by a racket of construction as a massive framework for a spandrel descends slowly to the floor. (p. 14.)

The visual is of course the rational sense par excellence: Krak's visual 'rape' of the hill is a far more effective form of violence than Stucley's botched assault on Cant. It penetrates analytically — the limestone, and imposes geometrical form — the arc. It is this that Ann instinctively recognises and her words again reinforce the affinity of female body and hill.

As Krak makes good his escape, a crack emerges in the women's unity. Skinner has heard Ann refer to her returned husband as physically 'beautiful', she freely admits that outwardly, at least, she finds him more attractive:

> SKINNER: You called him beautiful. Your husband. Beautiful, you said.
> ANN: He was. The bone has made an appearance. (Pause) Well, he is. HE IS. (p. 5.)

This is indicative of how Ann refuses to deny her own instinctive responses in the interests of personal or ideological commitment. She will not pacify the jealous Skinner by retracting or amending what she has said.

The remark is the hairline crack that opens up a gulf that finally overwhelms their love. Skinner's suspicion makes her ugly in Ann's eyes:

> ANN: You go so ugly, in a second, at the bid of a thought, so ugly. (p. 6.)

Taken with the line quoted above, this comment of Ann's is further indication of her tendency to value the aesthetic quality of pure appearances. Although the women seem reconciled, their separation has begun. It is interesting in that the feelings concerning the lost opportunity to kill Krak thereby preventing the castle — the 'fulcrum of disaster' — apply in exactly the same moment to their own relationship. Skinner, at any rate, explicitly states later that the castle and her love are one and the same.

In the dialogue that follows, Skinner talks volubly of their female society and their relationship; it is almost a monologue in that Ann only seems to absorb and humour her lover.

> SKINNER: *I helped your births. And your conceptions. Sat by the bedroom, at the door, while you took the man's thing in you, shuddering with disgust and trying hard to see it only as the mating of dumb cattle —*
> ANN: *It was –*
> SKINNER: *Yes, and I managed. I did manage. And washed you, and parted your hair. I never knew such intimacy, did you? Tell me, all this unity!*
> ANN: *Never — (pp. 6–7.)*

It emerges later that Skinner herself is barren — an irony, considering her militant espousal of nature, that nature should have denied her personal fertility. The womb is frequently seen as the uniquely female attribute which links woman to nature. Skinner, perhaps sensing an evasive complaisance in Ann, is determined to confront her:

> SKINNER: *...Europe is a million miles long, isn't it, how did they pick their way back here, AN ANT COULD PASS THROUGH A BONFIRE EASIER! (Ann laughs. SKINNER looks at her) How? (Pause)*
> ANN: *Why are you looking at me like that?*
> SKINNER: *How, then?*
> ANN: *I suppose because —*
> SKINNER: *You drew him. (Pause)*
> ANN: *What?*
> SKINNER: *Drew him. With your underneath. (Pause)*
> ANN: *I do think — if we —*
> SKINNER: *DOWN THERE CALLED TO HIM ACROSS THE SPACES!*
> ANN: *Look —*
> SKINNER: *I HATE GOD AND NATURE, THEY MADE US VIOLABLE AS BITCHES!*
> *(p. 7.)*

Skinner's espousal of feminist attitudes is very much a consciously willed gesture. She states earlier how she exerted all her witchcraft, her natural magic, to prevent the Crusaders returning. There is a sense, however, that she doubts profoundly what she professes most passionately and this contradiction emerges in her outburst here. She has little faith in the efficacy of her witchcraft. Her inclination to hate both 'God' and 'Nature', the latter the conventional feminist antithesis to the patriarchal deity, means that there is for her no ideological refuge in an alien universe. This intense feeling of exposure leads her to invest everything in her relationship with Ann. Her contention here, that Ann drew her husband back, is an accusation which is only consistent with the magical world of seduction implying as it does action at a distance and the **reversal of causality**: it would be reasonable to say that Stucley was drawn to his wife — she being the passive object; it is entirely irrational to argue that *'DOWN THERE CALLED TO HIM'*. Yet seduction does not absolve the passive object of complicity in seductive action. According to Baudrillard, to become object is the seductive strategy par excellence.[3] The subjective 'truth' of this can be evidenced in the 'irrational' guilt that one can experience at the death of close friends or relatives. Because no direct causal link can be established, reason insists that we dismiss such emotions even though the feelings are nevertheless 'real' enough. A similar, though less dramatic seductive reversal, is claimed by Stucley when he assaults Cant:

> STUCLEY: ....LOOK WHAT YOU'VE MADE ME DO!... (p. 4.)

The scene between Ann and Skinner is cut short by the arrival of Stucley. Skinner leaves and there follows a cataclysmic confrontation between husband and wife. The writing here represents an extraordinary achievement on Barker's part in showing a mind fighting disintegration in the face of catastrophe. As I have already observed. Stucley feels for his wife a quasi-religious devotion and he has been anticipating this moment for years. When he enters, carrying *'a white garment'* which he wishes her to put on, Ann dismisses Skinner with the injunction — *'Trust me'*. Stucley obviously hears this and part of his mind is disturbed:

> STUCLEY: *Trust you? Why? (He looks at her) You look so — (Pause) Trust you? Why? (Pause) Imagine what I — if you would condescend to — what I — the riot of my feelings when I look at — (Pause) Trust you to do what exactly? (Pause) In seven years I have aged twenty. And you, if anything, have grown younger, so we who were never boy and girl exactly have now met in some middling maturity, I have seen your face on tent roofs, don't laugh at me, will you? (Pause)*
> ANN: *No.*
> STUCLEY: *That is a ploughman's hag and you — what is it, exactly? (Pause) I found the church bunged up with cow and bird dung, the place we married in, really, what — (Pause) So I prayed in the nettles. (Pause) Very devout picture of young English warrior returning to his domain etcetera get your needle out and make a tapestry why don't you? Or don't you do that any more? (Pause) Christ knows what goes on here, you must explain to me over the hot milk at bedtime, everything changes and dreams are ballocks but you can't help dreaming, even knowing a dream is — (Pause) It is quite amusing coming back to this I was saying to the Arab every hundred yards I have this little paradise and he went mmm and mmm he knew the sardonic bastard, they are not romantic like us are they, muslims, and they're right! Please put this on because I —*
> ANN: *No. (Pause) (pp. 7–8.)*

The confrontation is a seductive duel — increasingly desperate on Stucley's part — as he struggles to engage Ann on a level which will reassure him that 'everything is as it was'. Her apparent passivity, and I have discussed

2.   'Put this on, please…' *The Castle*, Act I, Scene 1.

passivity above, is a strategy on her part which preserves her seductive enigma: she does not immediately present him with 'a position' — as Skinner would desire. She has already stated that she finds his appearance 'beautiful' — so there is an attraction on her part which is presumably what sustains his 'performance' in this 'moment' for so long. A directly comparable scene — to which I have already alluded — is to be found in the last of *The Possibilities* — *Not Him* where a 'wife' confronts a husband returning after years in the war: she remains veiled for much of the time and the central tension expressed in the title is the question of identity — in every sense the man is, paradoxically, both 'same' and 'other' an ambiguous quality which renders him sexually intensely desirable but simultaneously morally dispensable. Here the veil is suggested in Ann's silence and ambiguity.

To return to the passage quoted above, it can be seen that most of Stucley's pauses are invitations to Ann to intervene — invitations or perhaps temptations which, for the most part, she refuses. It is important that the confrontation is presented as genuinely dramatic — i.e. that Ann is, initially at least, 'open' to being seduced. The audience should have the feeling that Stucley might win and in a way this eventuality is heralded by Skinner's irrational accusation. A 'closed' performance from Ann would invalidate the scene. On his part, Stucley can be seen to be suspended between different levels which demand an extraordinary technical agility from the actor: there is the persistent nagging suspicion expressed in the *'Trust you? Why?'s*; this contrasts starkly with the rapture expressed in the other lines where Stucley assays to seduce Ann by performing his passion. He is well aware that one seduces with weakness and not only parades his vulnerability but draws attention to it — *'don't laugh at me, will you?'* This phrase is interesting in its possible resonances and ambiguities. It is in fact an invitation to Ann to do precisely that — laugh at him — though indulgently rather than derisively. The *'will you?'* can be read as a plea. For her to laugh in this way, would be to release the tension and to give him the reassurance he wants. Her *'No'*, though superficially accomodating his plea, positively reinforces the tension. It must be born in mind that every instance where Ann refuses a gesture of 'vulnerability' leaves Stucley terribly wounded and confused. At the same time it is highly likely that Ann also feels his pain but she must bluff and conceal any sympathy from him in order to preserve her strength.

This particular refusal causes him to recall his suspicion. He attempts pompously to gain the authority of the moral high ground with restrained indignation at the state of the church. When Ann does not respond, he immediately adjusts this with what is intended to be an attractive demonstration of humility and perhaps an element of pathos — *'So I prayed in the nettles.'* Her silence again undercuts his performance and leaves his gesture sadly exposed and ridiculous in its self-consciousness and calculation. Simply by not responding she imposes, yet does not impose, that meaning on him. He tries to retrieve the gesture and cover the wound by burlesquing himself — a frequent stratagem of his: *'Very devout picture....make a tapestry why don't you?'* As Stucley's agony continues, it becomes clear that he would be prepared to concede anything provided Ann still loved him. His comment about her explaining *'over the hot milk at bedtime'* amply illustrates his dependency. Her second *'No'* is a direct refusal to comply with his wishes. In the speech that follows, he tries to retrieve their relationship by recalling their wedding night, going on to describe how he has carried her image like a shrine in his heart through all the horrors and degradations of war:

> STUCLEY: *... what we did in Hungary I would not horrify you with — they got more barmy by the hour. Not me, though. I thought she'll take my bleeding feet in her warm place, she'll lay me down in clean sheets and work warm oils into my skin and food, we'll spend whole days at — but everything is contrary, must be, mustn't it, I who jumped in every pond of murder kept this one thing pure in my head, pictured you half-naked on an English night, your skin which was translucent from one angle and deep-furrowed from another, your odour even which I caught once in the middle of a scrap, do you believe that, even smells are stored. I'm sorry I chucked your loom out of the window, amazing strength comes out of temper, it's half a ton that thing if it's — trust me, what does that mean? (p. 8.)*

One of the aspects of Stucley's character, his sense of identity, which needs to be noted concerns social class: he is self-consciously upper class, very much in the 'stiff upper lip' English public school mode, an influence which also finds expression in some of his more childish behaviour. Later in the play, when he begins seriously to regress, this becomes increasingly obvious:

> STUCLEY: *... Gang meets at sunset by the camp! The password is — (He whispers in KRAK's ear) DON'T TELL! (He goes to leave) Gang meets at sunset and no girls!... (p. 30.)*

> STUCLEY: *... Play snowballs with me! I did love boyhood more than anything! Play snowballs! (p. 25.)*

The latter request is also addressed to Krak and indicates how Stucley, having failed disastrously with women and sexuality, yearns for the simple pre-pubertal male companionship of 'school'. In the context of the Crusades, such references are of course strictly prochronistic but are entirely consistent with Barker's dramatic method.

Returning to Stucley's confrontation with Ann, this sense of superior identity reasserts itself like a tic in the phrase *'Not me, though'* which he repeats four times in this scene. This is a superiority, as the context of the phrase invariably implies, founded in a rigorous self-control. Class is also evident in his disparaging reference to Skinner as *'a ploughman's hag'* and it even enters his relationship with his wife: earlier, when he rushed off anticipating catching her in confusion, he imagined her saying *'Oh, my lord'*. The language of the fantasy he expresses here — *'I thought she'll take my bleeding feet in her warm place, she'll lay me down in clean sheets and work warm oils into my skin…'* carries Biblical connotations, specifically of Mary Magdalene and Christ, a theme which returns later. (It is not difficult to understand why Ann does not want to continue the marriage!) The *'pond of murder'* image is equally eloquent: the two concepts are not linked in any obvious way — a pond connoting stillness rather than the violence associated with murder. The image reflects Stucley's psychology — what he does not see is that he brings the violence to the pond by jumping into it; as a gesture it also expresses a Canute-like fatuity. The reference to Ann's skin as *'deep-furrowed'* again reinforces the affinity of woman and earth. Stucley's apology for the loom is yet another desperate climb-down which serves to emphasise his abjection.

It is at this point that Ann utters her first sentence of the encounter; it is highly significant and decisive:

> ANN: *You've not changed. Thinner, but the same. For all the marching and the stabbing. Whereas quietly, here I have. (p. 8.)*

It is as if she had been assessing him while he spoke and had finally come to a decision. She had been interested in the physical difference, finding it attractive, and was obviously curious to know if his personality had altered. Ann has, presumably, decided in embarking upon her relationship with Skinner to abandon the husband she knew before the war; the only question that might arise would be whether this was the 'same' man. She concludes that it is and that her decision will therefore stand.

She proceeds without delay to tell him that she has not reciprocated his fidelity. Barker's stage directions indicate again his fascination for the moment of catastrophe:

> ANN: *No. (Pause. He is suspended between hysteria and disbelief) (p. 9.)*

The 'suspension', however, does not last long before giving way to full-blown hysteria. Stucley finds in this moment a revelation of universal scale. All of his experience is suddenly illuminated by a shattering light:

> STUCLEY: *I think when God says — CRUSH THIS BASTARD — I wish there was a priest here, but there isn't so I offer you my version, you hark to my theology — he really is the most*

> *THOROUGHGOING OF ALL DEITIES, no wonder we all bow down to him his grasp of pain and pressure is so exquisite and all-comprehending… And I have just fought the Holy War on His behalf! Oh, Lord and Master of Cruelty, who has no shred of mercy for thy servants, I worship thee! (p. 9.)*

As Ann proceeds to confirm his worst fears, his view of the deity is simultaneously strengthened:

> STUCLEY: *… now tell me she has children by the very interlopers who greeted me as I climbed my very own steps.*
> ANN: *Yes.*
> STUCLEY: *Yes! Yes! I know the source of our religion! It is that He in His savagery is both excessive and remorseless and to our shrieks both deaf and blind! (p. 9.)*

Stucley's excesses can appear comical to an audience, but it is important that the performer should not play this up. His words here are not 'mere rhetoric', hysterical exaggerations; they are borne out in his subsequent behaviour. The actor playing Stucley needs to counterbalance the potentially ludicrous with a strong sense of the man's terrible pain. There is a tendency to dismiss his claims because they are obviously 'irrational' and 'the balance of his mind' is clearly disturbed. Yet the world of *The Castle* and Barker's plays in general, is not rational: it is seductive and fatal. Baudrillard:

> *The power of events that happen to you without your having willed them, without your having anything to do with it. But not by chance. They happen, and this coincidence touches you, it's destined for you. Even if you didn't want it, because you didn't want it, you're seduced by it. That's the whole difference between destiny and chance. For pure chance, even supposing that it exists, is entirely indifferent to us; pure occurrence has nothing seductive about it for us — it's objective, period. It is the strategy of chance we adopt to neutralize an event or attenuate its effect: 'It happened by chance' (Not my doing)……. And here chance is quite helpful: it's enough to think (difficult as that is) that things happen without reason, or for a maximum of objective reasons (technical, material, statistical) that remove the responsibility from us, and which, in fact, absolve us from whatever the event could contain of a profoundly seductive nature, whose cause we might have wanted to be…[4]*

It is in this way that the rational world of 'reality' is reassuring: reassurance, however, comes at a price because this draining off of the world's symbolic potency reduces what is left to grey banality.

> *Thus from a moral point of view, we may want to protect ourself by all sorts of alibis (including chance), from the fatal interconnections of events, but from a symbolic perspective it is deeply repugnant to have a neutral world, ruled by chance and thus innocuous and meaningless, and similarly for a world ruled by objective causes; neither one, although easier to live, can resist the fascinating imagination of a universe entirely ruled by a divine or diabolical chain of **willed** coincidences, that is, a universe where we seduce events, where*

we induce them and make them happen by the omnipotence of thought — a cruel universe where no one is innocent, and especially not us, a universe where our subjectivity has dissolved (and we joyously accept it) because it has been absorbed into the automatism of events, into their objective unfolding. It has in some way become a world.[5]

In a rational world, the world of 'reality', the fact for instance that Stucley had thrown his knife into the bushes during his previous encounter with Cant thereby rendering it unavailable for stabbing his wife now, would be ascribed to Chance. Chance, however, is not possible in seduction where everything that happens is destiny. Stucley, who believes in power, must make sense of why an all-powerful deity chooses to treat him in this way. His strategy is to 'joyously accept' his pain, a seductive reversal; in gleefully anticipating new horrors, humiliations and frustrations which subsequently prove correct, he experiences the exhilaration of racing ahead of 'the mind of God'; he 'understands' God and has the satisfaction of willing events, — as he says later, on the discovery of a rival castle:

> STUCLEY: *Everything I fear, it comes to pass. Everything I imagine is vindicated. Awful talent I possess. DON'T I HAVE AN AWFUL TALENT? TALENT?* (p. 34.)

When, therefore, he has exhausted his hysteria and regained his self-control, he becomes — in a godlike way — cruel. He considers the possibility of cold-bloodedly murdering Ann:

> STUCLEY: *...I could kill you and no one would bat an eyelid.* (p. 9.)

She still feels that she can influence him and suggests that he goes away. He bluffs giving her suggestion reasonable consideration:

> ANN: *Don't stay.*
> STUCLEY: *Don't stay?*
> ANN: *No. Be welcome, and pass through.*
> STUCLEY: *One night and then —*
> ANN: *Yes.*
> STUCLEY: *What — in the stable, kip down and —*
> ANN: *Not in the stable.*
> STUCLEY: *Not in the stable? You mean I might —*
> ANN: *Don't, please, become sarcastic, it —*
> STUCLEY: *Inside the house, perhaps, we might just —*
> ANN: *Useless sarcasm, it —*
> STUCLEY: *Under the stairs and creep away at first light —*
> ANN: *Undermines your honour —*
> STUCLEY: *WHAT HONOUR YOU DISHEVELLED AND IMPERTINENT SLAG.* (Pause) *You see, you make me lose my temper, you make me abusive, why not stay, it is my home.* (pp. 9–10.)

Here, Stucley has acquired a sufficient degree of detachment and self-control to be able to play with Ann's seriousness. The moment she realises he is doing this she attempts to use his sense of '*honour*' to subdue him. He rebuts this tactic by highlighting her hypocrisy in attempting to use it: the epithet '*dishevelled*' no doubt refers to her appearance, particularly her hair (much reference is made to her '*plaits*' in the course of the action). She attempts to challenge Stucley with the suggestion that he should simply go away:

> ANN: *Go on.*
> STUCLEY: *To where?*
> ANN: *The horizon.*
> STUCLEY: *I own the horizon.*
> ANN: *Cross it then. (Pause) I'm cruel, but I do it to be simple. To cut off hopes cleanly. No tearing wounds, I'm sorry if your dreams are spoiled but —*
> STUCLEY: *It is perfectly kind of you —*
> ANN: *Not kind —*
> STUCLEY: *Yes, perfectly kind and typically considerate of you, I do appreciate the instinct but —*
> ANN: *Not kind, I say —*
> STUCLEY: *YES! Down on your knees, now.*
> ANN: *What —*
> STUCLEY: *On your knees, now —*
> ANN: *Are you going to be —*
> STUCLEY: *Down, now —*
> ANN: *Childish and —*
> STUCLEY: *Yes, I WAS YOUR CHILD, WASN'T I? (Pause, He suddenly weeps. She watches him, then goes to him. He embraces her, then thrusts her away) PENITENCE FOR ADULTERY! (p. 10.)*

Ann's suggestion here is an important article of faith with her: she believes that it is always possible 'to pass on', to begin again somewhere else; she has faith in the permanent possibility of 'the other' — other places, other times, other people — which is integral to her open, seductive nature. Later she gives to the horribly tortured Skinner the same advice as she offers here to her husband. She herself, pregnant with Krak's child, pleads with him to leave the castle and 'go on over the horizon' with her. He tells her that there is nowhere to go to escape the castle and this brings about her suicide. Her final words —

> ANN: *… (Pause. She looks at Krak) There is nowhere except where you are. Correct. Thank you. If it happens somewhere, it will happen everywhere. There is nowhere except where you are. Thank you for truth. (Pause. She kneels, pulls out a knife) Bring it down. All this. (p. 39.)*

Stucley again plays with her sincerity, emphasising her kindness. It is clear, however, that he is now concerned merely with appearances and with power. He insists — against Ann's sincerity — that she is being kind — the appearance of kindness. He also tries to insist on the appearance of submission to his will — the kneeling. Her accusation of childishness causes him to confront her — and simultaneously perhaps himself — with the truth about their relationship — *'I WAS YOUR CHILD, WASN'T I?'*. She does not answer his question — tacitly admitting that he was. This revelation is a further blow and he collapses in tears, first instinctively seeking, then refusing the maternal comfort she offers.

Barker prefaces the title page of *The Castle* with the question — 'What is Politics, but the absence of Desire …?' When Stucley's desire is violently checked in this scene, he reverts abruptly to power and is seduced by the playful quality in power which is cruelty. His failure to enforce submission on Ann is followed immediately by the arrival of Hush — a decrepid octogenarian left behind by the Crusaders who has been used by the women to father the children of their new commonwealth. He forces Hush to kneel and confess his sins to his lord:

> STUCLEY: … *Kiss my hands and tell me what you did against me. The more extravagant, the more credence I attach to it, promise you.*
> HUSH: *I did not praise you in your absence.*
> STUCLEY: *Oh, that's nothing, you mean you abused me, surely?*
> HUSH: *Abused you, yes.*
> STUCLEY: *Excellent, go on.*
> ANN: *This is disgusting.*
> STUCLEY: *Disgusting? No, he longs for his confession!* (p. 11.)

In Hush, Stucley has found a subordinate who is prepared to be totally obsequious and say whatever he wants to hear. He is satisfied with appearances. Ann is horrified; the women have accorded dignity and respect to every individual, besides she is concerned that he will confess his sexual intercourse with her. Hush eventually, at Stucley's direct prompting, admits to precisely this but, ironically, he is not believed:

> HUSH: *I lay on her and on others naked and did put my seed in them and —*
> STUCLEY: *Oh, rubbish, it's beyond belief. I hate bad lies, lies that fall apart, there's no entertainment in them.* (p. 11.)

The truth or falsity of Hush's confessions is not the significant feature for Stucley: what concerns him in his world of appearances is the purely seductive quality of those appearances. It is interesting that Hush finds Stucley's mistreatment of him refreshing:

> *HUSH: Thank you.*
> *STUCLEY: Thank me, why?*
> *HUSH: Because the worst thing in age is the respect. The smile of condescension, and the*
> *hush with which the most banal opinion is received. The old know nothing. Fling them down.*
> *They made the world and they need punishing. (p. 11.)*

Or is this merely a bluff on his part, designed to endear him to Stucley? (Who does in fact respond with some signs of affection.) The latter's exit lines express his new resolution:

> *STUCLEY: I cherish nothing, cherishing's out, and what was soft in me has liquified into a*
> *posion puddle. Not to be fooled. That's my dream now, THANK YOU, UNIVERSE! (Pause)*
> *Educated me. Educated me... (He goes out) (p. 12.)*

His words here reflect the acceptance of the cruel universe indicated earlier in the scene. This confrontation between Stucley and Ann is of crucial importance to the development of the action leading on directly in the following scene to the building of the castle — an action clearly linked to the former's state of mind.

The scene ends with Ann briefly upbraiding Hush because she feels he will do or say anything in order to continue his existence and is appalled at his lack of moral sense:

> *ANN: Why do you love your life so much? (He stops) So much that even dignity gets spewed,*
> *and truth kicked into blubber, and will itself as pliable as a string of gut? You have no appetite*
> *but life itself, I mean breathing and continuing. (He shrugs) There can't be a man alive with*
> *more children and less interest in the world they grow up in. (p. 12.)*

She herself has had the courage to face up to Stucley and defy him — which could easily have cost her her life. She is concerned naturally that her husband should not be able to reimpose his former authority. Hush's apparent will to self-subjection, however, is inauspicious in this respect. Her words remind one of the notion that the traditional role of women in the nurture of children predisposes them to having a wider moral concern than men. Her parting shot at Hush expresses a strong resentment of injustice which nevertheless strikes a characteristically 'matronising' note:

> *IF YOU ACHIEVE IMMORTALITY I SHALL BE FURIOUS. (p. 12.)*

Scene Two begins with Batter telling another aged sycophant, Sponge, about his relationship with Krak. Batter is a thug who glories in his own violence but is strangely fascinated by the intellectual engineer. He feels a sense of proprietorship about the Arab whom he personally saved from slaughter:

BATTER: … And he is mine, in all his rareness, mine, as if I'd birthed him, yes, DON'T LOOK AT ME LIKE THAT, I am his second mother! (p. 12.)

He describes how he was engaged in an orgy of violence after entering Jerusalem — sparing no one. Suddenly he encountered Krak:

BATTER: … And he stared into the little lights of what must have been — my kindness — and I stopped, the dagger in my hand tipped this way … and that … slippery in my fist. I pondered. AFTER EIGHTEEN STAIRCASES OF MURDER … and of course, because I pondered, the genius was safe. Funny. Funny that I pondered when this was the very bugger who designed the fort… (p. 13.)

Batter is describing a moment of pure seduction. His action, in *'pondering'*, is a mystery to him. Krak had apparently touched a quality hitherto completely repressed, something he was wholly unaware of within himself — his *'kindness'*; this again is the kind of reversal which is typical of seduction. It is interesting that Batter thinks of this moment as a birth — as if the old Krak had died and a new one been reborn in that instant; certainly the moment marked the commencement of a new life for Krak and symbolically the character presented in the play is the child of death and destruction. Later in the play, Ann tells him that he needs to be born yet again:

ANN: It is you that needs to be born. I will be your midwife. Through the darkness, down the black canal — (p. 35.)

Batter's present infatuation for Krak is based upon his profound respect for his violence — a violence he recognises as being far superior to his own.

After Stucley has dragged in and dusted off his lapsed priest, Nailer, sending him to clean the church, Krak reveals his plan for the castle. This, again, is a crucial seductive moment:

STUCLEY: … Go on …(Krak holds out a large sheet of paper) Has he made a drawing for me? (He smiles) He has … (He looks at Krak beaming) The Great Amazer! (He takes it, looks at it) Which way up is it? (He turns it round and round) I genuflect before the hieroglyphs but what —
KRAK: No place is not watched by another place. (STUCLEY nods) The heights are actually depths.
STUCLEY: Yup.
KRAK: The weak points are actually strong points.
STUCLEY: Yup.
KRAK: The entrances are exits.
STUCLEY: Yes!
KRAK: The doors lead into pits.
STUCLEY: Go on!
KRAK: It resembles a defence but is really an attack.

STUCLEY: Yes —
KRAK: It cannot be destroyed.
STUCLEY: Mmm —
KRAK: Therefore it is a threat —
STUCLEY: Mmm —
KRAK: It will makes enemies where there are none —
STUCLEY: You're losing me —
KRAK: It makes war necessary — (STUCLEY looks at him) It is the best thing I have ever done.
(STUCLEY's long stare is interrupted by a racket of construction as a massive framework for a spandrel descends slowly to the floor.) (p. 14.)

The significance of this castle is emphasised by the title of the play and during the course of the action it is physically built on stage: a prominence not often given to a physical object in Barker; I have asserted that his drama follows the Szondi model of interpersonal action which seeks in general to banish the world of objects. *The Castle* is not a serious exception and, if anything, serves to reinforce the essentially interpersonal focus of his work because the castle in question is first and foremost a mental phenomenon. It arises from and constitutes the interrelations of the characters. This is not to suggest that the castle is not a 'thing in itself'; it certainly has a kind of identity. In discussing the focus of Barker's dramaturgy, I have advanced the view that the essential reference point of the 'interpersonal' is not the 'personal' but the 'inter' and the castle is such an 'inter' — a complex but nevertheless identifiable force field of negative energies. The sudden appearance of the castle here emphasises simultaneously both its insubstantial/magical quality and its substance: an ambiguity which adds to its seductive potency; it is summoned out of nowhere in response to a profound impulse of the human mind.

Stucley, as we have seen, is bent on a cruel dominance and the castle recommends itself to him for this reason. Historically, Barker is suggesting the castle of the Norman barons: not a system of communal defence like the Celtic or Saxon hill forts. But an alien imposition, offensive, the property of a private individual, the function of which was to dominate and exploit the land. According to Professor R. Allen Brown:

> there is no doubt that castles stood for lordship in men's minds and were the expression as well as much of the substance of lordly power and control.[6]

The castle enabled this dominance to be achieved by a relatively small elite of armoured cavalry:

> Because of the developing strength of fortification, because throughout the period of the castle's ascendancy defence was in the ascendant over attack, garrisons could be and

3. *The Castle.*

were comparatively small; yet that small force could and did hold the district in which it was based unless it was locked up by a full-scale and prolonged investment involving a far greater force...[7]

The fact that the castle was also a residence (and in the post-medieval world this became its principal function) has tended to obscure from a modern perspective some of its more brutal aspects — of which the Anglo-Saxon Chronicle provides eloquent testimony:

For every great man built him castles and held them against the king; and they filled the whole land with these castles. They sorely burdened the unhappy people of the country with forced labour on the castles; and when the castles were built they filled them with devils and wicked men. By night and by day they seized those whom they believed to have any wealth, whether they were men or women; and in order to get their gold and silver, they put them into prison and tortured them with unspeakable tortures, for never were martyrs tortured as they were. They hung them up by the feet and smoked them with foul smoke. They strung them up by the thumbs or by the head, and hung coats of mail on their feet. They tied knotted cords round their heads and twisted it till it entered the brain. They put them in dungeons wherein were adders and snakes and toads, and so destroyed them.[8]

Barker's castle draws upon all of these conventional historical functions and associations, yet its initial impact upon Stucley is manifestly seductive. In the first place, he is fascinated by Krak's intellectual power — *'The Great Amazer'* but does not understand the drawing. Krak elucidates, moving from concrete particularities to abstract generalities. Barker expresses the seduction in a kind of stichomythia which, instead of conveying conflict as is usual in classical drama, draws the characters together in an escalating vertigo of enthusiasm — Krak for his creativity and Stucley for the power it offers. It is significant the latter does not understand the wider implications of the edifice — *'You're losing me —'*. All of Krak's comments can be seen to refer directly to particular physical attributes of the medieval castle but Barker does also intend that the 'definition' should have wider resonance. Hence *'No place is not watched by another place'* suggests the mass surveillance of totalitarianism. His comments about *'heights'*, *'weak points'*, and *'entrances'*, are all reversals, with the weakness/strength antithesis particularly associated with seduction. The castle is a labyrinth of deception and bluff. But, perhaps above all else and for Stucley in particular, it holds all the fascination of an enigma.

In this respect (its seductive, deceptive, enigmatic qualities), Barker's castle partakes of the nature of Kafka's castle in the novel of the same name. There, the central figure, Joseph K, arrives in a small town which is entirely dominated by a mysterious and sinister bureaucracy lodged in the castle; he becomes enmeshed in an entirely irrational seductive duel with this authority, a game of bluff and counterbluff, fought out through a series of endless intermediaries. In typical seductive fashion, K's aim, if it ever existed, is lost in the fascination of the duel and the inexorability of the next move. In this sense, Barker's castle, like Kafka's, suggests a model of the more contemporary state, the origins of which literally date back to the castle society of William the Conqueror. It symbolises politics. At the time of the play's first production, the castle was widely seen as a metaphor for the Cold War arms race which had intensified under Reagan; in this respect the constant need to improve and extend the castle, the way it seemed to draw everything else into its orbit, its growing threat of total armageddon (as manifested in Skinner's vision at the end of Act 1) bore out this particular connection, — as do Krak's comments that the castle will serve to make enemies where there are none and will make war necessary. Having said this, the castle is nevertheless a symbol which develops with the action of the play in the direction of less conventional associations.

Very shortly after the sudden and dramatic arrival of the beginnings of the castle, Skinner appears, *'draped in flowers'*. She attempts to challenge Krak, as author of the castle, urging him to look at the *'superior geometry'* of a flower. She is simply ignored both by him and Holiday; her 'feminist' protest is brushed aside. She reacts with anger:

> SKINNER: ... — *all right, don't look at it, why should I save you, why should I educate you* — (p. 15.)

The antithesis here between a masculine culture of rationality (Krak's sharp, hard instruments) and a feminine one of nature and instinct is emphasised by Skinner; however, the manifest failure of her protest causes her to harden and she menacingly threatens Holiday with her witchcraft. Her instinct is to reject the male altogether. With the arrival of brute force in the shape of Batter, she departs with a gesture of contempt — she flings up her skirts and shows her arse.

Batter and Holiday consider her, and their language again connects the female body with the land:

> HOLIDAY: ... *are these towers really going to be ninety foot above the curtain? I don't complain, every slab is food and drink to me, but ninety foot? Who are you — it's a quiet country what I see of it — no, the woman's touched, surely?*
> BATTER: (contemplatively) *Skinner's arse ...*
> HOLIDAY: *What?*
> BATTER: *He told me how he lay upon that arse, and she kept stiff as rock, neither moaning nor moving, but rock. So when the bishop asked for soldiers he was first forward, to get shot of her with Christ's permission. (p. 16.)*

Krak has seen the hill as 'an arc of pure limestone'; Ann had described her 'soft' as going 'rigid' at the sight of the engineer; rock was, of course, the ideal site for a castle because of the difficulty in undermining it. The implication here is that the castle is not purely and simply a product of the masculine but that the resistant feminine is also involved. Significantly and ironically, both Skinner and her husband find in the figure of Christ a solution to their sexual problems.

Holiday attempts to quiz Krak about the design of the castle but is met with silence and goes back to work. Batter has watched this non-exchange and continues to watch Krak who, for the first time, responds by stating his own feelings:

> KRAK: *Dialogue is not a right, is it? When idiots waylay geniuses, where is the obligation? (Pause) And words, like buckets, slop with meanings. (Pause) To talk, what is that but the exchange of clumsy approximations, the false endeavour to share knowledge, the false endeavour to disseminate truths arrived at in seclusion? (Pause) When the majority are, perceptibly, incapable of the simplest intellectual discipline, what is the virtue of incessant speech? The whole of life serves to remind us we exist among inert banality. (Pause) I only state the obvious. The obvious being the starting point of architecture, as of any other science... (p. 16.)*

Krak uses his silence to preserve his emotional detachment from the world in which he finds himself. His intellectual supremacy and pride in his reason allows him to dismiss others contemptuously as '*idiots*'. Reason does not recognise the 'other' as such since everything in the universe is reducible to its own laws. As a rationalist, he finds verbal communication particularly distasteful because words are never merely definitive — they connote and can, at worst, be ambiguous. His world is secluded — even solipsistic ('*we exist among inert banality*') and this, according to Levinas, is the very world of Reason itself, a world which must exclude and repress all forms of seduction with its irrational magic. As we discover later, Krak's rationalism is also an alibi: the life among '*inert banality*' may be sterile and grey — as Baudrillard says:

> *from a symbolic perspective it is deeply repugnant to have a neutral world, ruled by chance and thus innocuous and meaningless, and similarly for a world ruled by objective causes;*[9]

On the other hand this view does, according to Baudrillard —

> *...absolve us from whatever the event could contain of a profoundly seductive nature, whose cause we might have wanted to be.*[10]

We see later that Krak's attitude has helped him to repress, to some extent at least, his emotional responses to the horrific butchery of his entire family. His character is as much in a state of violent reaction as Stucley's or Skinner's. It is necessary to point out, however, that Krak's scientific detachment here is also a performance for the benefit of his admirer, Batter, from whom he is consciously concealing a personal commitment — the destruction of his captors. Conceivably, this is the enigma which renders him such a fascinating figure to both Stucley and Batter.

The following scene, Scene 3, begins with Skinner physically tackling Cant whom she has caught having sex with one of the bricklayers. Cant describes her predicament:

> *CANT: … It was easy before the builders come, but there are dozens of these geezers and they*
> *— I gaze at their trousers, honestly I do, whilst thinking, enemy, enemy! I do gaze so, though*
> *hating myself, obviously … (p. 17.)*

Skinner feels that she should be punished but Ann finds Skinner's anger excessive:

> *SKINNER: … We have done such things here and they come back and straddle us, where is*
> *the strength if we go up against the wall skirts up and occupied like that? (Pause) I do think, I*
> *do think, to understand is not to condone, is it? (Pause) I do feel so alone, do you feel that?*
> *(Pause) It always rains here, which we loved once. I love you and I wish we could just love,*
> *but no, this is the test, all love is tested, or else it cannot know its power…*
> *CANT: I'm sorry. (p. 18.)*

The problem for the women is power; Skinner begins here to insist on the 'power' of 'love', on 'strength'; crucially, she accepts the challenge posed by the castle, seeing it as a 'test' of their love. On the other hand, she has moments when she wishes things were as before, and when she says here that she feels alone, she indicates a profound doubt about Ann's love. She does, however, see clearly the long term implications of the castle:

> *SKINNER: Where there are builders, there are whores, and where there are whores, there are*
> *criminals, and after the criminals come the police, the great heap heaving, and what was peace*
> *and simple is dirt and struggle, and where there was a field to stand up straight in there is*
> *loud and frantic city. Stucley will make a city of this valley, what does he say to you?*
> *ANN: Nothing. (p. 18.)*

Ann's lack of response in this scene is similar to her behaviour with Stucley. Like Stucley, Skinner is persistently attempting to probe and elicit reassurances which are not forthcoming. Like Stucley, she is continually forced to control her emotions:

> *SKINNER: Angry? Me? What? Mustn't be angry, no, be good, Skinner, be tolerant…*
> *(p. 18.)*

Eventually Skinner confronts Ann directly:

> SKINNER: ... *I WOULD RATHER YOU WERE DEAD THAN TOOK A STEP OR*
> *SHUFFLE BACK FROM ME. Dead, and I would do it. There I go, WHAT IS IT YOU*
> *LOOK SO DISTANT.*
> ANN: *I think you are — obsessive. (Pause)*
> SKINNER: *Obsessive, me? Obsessive? (Pause. She fights down something) I nearly got*
> *angry, then and nearly went — no — I will not — and — wait, the anger sinks — (Pause)*
> *Like tipping water on the sand, the anger goes, the anger vanishes — into what? I've no*
> *idea, my entrails, I assume. I do piss anger in the night, my pot is angerfull. (Pause) I am*
> *obsessive, why aren't you? (Pause) Every stone they raise is aimed at us. And things*
> *we have not dreamed of yet will come from it. Poems, love and gardening will be — and*
> *where you turn your eyes will be — and even the little middle of your heart which you*
> *think is your safe and actual self will be — transformed by it. I don't know how but even*
> *the way you plait your hair will be determined by it, and what we crop and even the colour*
> *of the babies, I do think its odd, so odd, that when you resist you are obsessive but when*
> *you succumb you are not WHOSE OBSESSION IS THIS THING or did you mean my*
> *love, they are the same thing actually. (Pause) They have a corridor of dungeons and*
> *somewhere are the occupants, they do not know yet and she fucked in there, not knowing it,*
> *of course, not being a witch could not imagine far enough, it is the pain of witches to see*
> *to the very end of things ... (p. 19.)*

Apart from showing the intensity of Skinner's passion for Ann, there are a number of noteworthy points in this quotation. Firstly Skinner is fully aware of the extent to which the castle will transform everything — *'even the little middle of your heart'* — in which case their love will not survive in its present form. Secondly, Skinner assumes initially that Ann is objecting to her obsession with the castle; it only occurs to her later that she could be referring to the quality of her love — *'or did you mean my love'*. What is interesting is that she declares them to be the same thing. Her love for Ann has become indistinguishable from her resistance to the castle. As a seductive personality, Ann perceives Skinner's resistance — in other words her commitment to sustaining particular truths in a hostile environment — as being *'obsessive'*. The use of this pejorative word serves yet again to underline their characteristic differences. Skinner also connects the dungeons here with sexuality of a brutal and loveless kind — *'fucked in there'*; this is a theme which will be developed later.

The crucial issue which separates the women concerns the most effective way of proceeding: Ann believes she must continue to talk to her husband whereas Skinner thinks there can be no talk between man and woman. Seduction, as far as she is concerned, is mere exploitation with the woman as victim:

> SKINNER: *... No talking. Words, yes, the patter and the eyes on your belt — (p. 19.)*

The distinction she makes here is between a full speech, face to face, and an indirect, manipulative and, ultimately, coercive communication. Skinner is also concerned about Ann having contact with her husband or men in general: she shows this again at the end of the scene when Ann tries to talk to Krak who appears from the shadows of his creation:

> ANN: *Have you no children? I somehow think you have not looked in children's eyes —*
> SKINNER: *DO YOU THINK HE LISTENS TO THAT MAWKISHNESS? (Pause)*
> KRAK: *Children? Dead or alive? (p. 20.)*

This is the beginning of Ann's attempt to seduce Krak which, as a strategy, proves to be more effective than Skinner's confrontation. The challenge which Krak poses Ann is that of awakening his humanity, — of discovering his '*kindness*', just as he, in his extremity, found Batter's. Though Krak's response here is intended to be disparaging, he does at least respond — divulging personal information and emotion — and Skinner's claim that he does not listen is refuted. Both Krak and Skinner found their identities on maintaining a contract — on resistance to seduction and change; Skinner asserts the permanence of her bond with Ann:

> SKINNER: *… I am in the grip of this eccentric view that sworn love is binding —*
> *(KRAK steps out of the shadows.)*
> KRAK: *Why not? If sworn hatred is. (p. 20.)*

Krak's contract, concealed in and by his '*reason*', is with his butchered family — for vengeance on his captors. Ann, on the other hand, can be seen continually to evade this kind of commitment , an evasion which manifests itself in her evasion of language, her avoidance of speech: she tells Skinner to '*trust*' her, to '*trust signs*'; as Stucley says:

> STUCLEY: *… trust me, what does that mean? (p. 8.)*

Act 1 Scene 4 is principally concerned with Stucley's doctrinal reorganisation of religion in the light of his sufferings during the Crusades and the insights we have seen him pluck from the adversities of his homecoming. It will be recalled that he had concluded that God was a sadist. Stucley, as a lord, has the power to re-establish his domain, his world, to accord with his own particular sensibilities. Reactions to this scene tend to be extreme — some find it shockingly blasphemous, others grotesquely comical; the scene is not constructed, however, with sensationalism in mind — the action here is a logical growth from what has preceded it. Things begin dramatically enough with Stucley entering to the praying figure of a recanted Nailer:

> *STUCLEY: Christ's cock.*
> *NAILER: Yes …?*
> *STUCLEY: IS NOWHERE MENTIONED! (He flings the Bible at him. NAILER ducks)*
> *NAILER: No…*
> *STUCLEY: Nor the cocks of his disciples.*
> *NAILER: No…*
> *STUCLEY: Peculiar. (p. 20.)*

Stucley takes up the conventional view of Christ as the deity made flesh, as the link whereby humanity may be reconciled with its creator — Christ as both fully man and God. Stucley, through sexuality, has known pain and ecstasy; he says —

> *STUCLEY: … The deity made manifest knows neither pain nor ecstasy, what use is He?*

> *STUCLEY: … this Christ who never suffered for a woman, who never felt the feeling which MAKES NO SENSE. (Pause) He can lend no comfort who has not been all the places that we have. (p. 21.)*

He is unable to identify with an asexual Christ and at this particular moment he feels the need for religious consolation, sublimating his thwarted desires. He has decided that Christ *'slagged Magdalene'* but that all references to his sexuality have been deleted from the Bible by *'neutered bishops'*. He orders Nailer to write the 'true' account of Christ and Magdalene according to his dictation:

> *STUCLEY: Yes, this is the Gospel of the Christ Erect! (He is inspired again) And by His gentleness, touches her heart, like any maiden rescued from the dragon gratitude stirs in her womb, she becomes to him the possibility of shared oblivion, she sheds all sin, and He experiences the — IRRATIONAL MANIFESTATIONS OF PITY WHICH IS — (Pause. He looks at NAILER, scrawling) Tumescence… (Pause) Got that?*
> *NAILER: Yes…*
> *STUCLEY: Now, we are closer to a man we understand, for at this moment of desire, Christ knows the common lot. (Pause) And she is sterile.*
> *NAILER: Sterile?*
> *STUCLEY: Diseased beyond conception, yes. So that they find, in passion, also tragedy …*
> *(NAILER catches up, looks at STUCLEY) What use is a Christ who has not suffered everything? (He wanders a little) They say the Jews killed Christ, but that's nonsense, the Almighty did. Why, did you say?*
> *NAILER: Yes…*
> *STUCLEY: Because His son discovered comfort. 'Oh, Father, why hast thou forsaken me?' Because in the body of the Magdalene He found the single place in which the madness of his father's world might be subdued. Unforgivable transgression the Lunatic could not forgive… (Pause. STUCLEY is moved by his own perceptions. He dries his eyes) You see how once Christ is restored to cock, all contradictions are resolved…*
> *NAILER: The Church of Christ the Lover… (p. 22.)*

Stucley's version naturally insists on a male dominance: Christ's attraction for Magdalene is described as the irrational manifestation of pity, — irrational because the seductive relation involves the element of weakness subduing strength; this relation is seen as redeeming the woman — *'she sheds all sin'*. His addition of sterility is again relevant to his own case but, notably, he fastens the blame for this on the woman (Ann, though childless with him, has had children while he was away). All of this describes his perception of himself up until his homecoming when the Lunatic/Cruel Father jealously murdered His son — Stucley/Christ for having discovered *'the single place in which the madness of his father's world might be subdued'*. Stucley's emphasis on the physicality of sex — *'cock'*, *'erect'*, *'tumescence'*, — serves to underline the conventionally Freudian analogy of this with the 'erection' of the castle. (Skinner talked in Scene 3 of the men 'boring into' the (feminine) 'hill'.) Both 'erections' — physical and theological — go together to form a system of total mental and physical domination; Stucley makes this clear when he ordains Nailer bishop by placing a tool bag on his head and tells him to go out and preach:

> STUCLEY: ... *No, I mean invoke Christ the Lover round the estate. I mean increase the yield of the demesne and plant more acres. Plough the woods. I want a further hour off them, with Christ's encouragement, say Friday nights — (p. 23.)*

This apparent cynicism in no way invalidates Stucley's own religious feelings: the Church of Christ the Lover is not solely intended as an instrument of exploitation though obviously it lends itself to this and as such he finds it useful.

When Ann enters, significantly, Stucley finds it necessary to flaunt his success with the castle:

> STUCLEY: ...*(Ann enters. He turns on her) We have the keep up to your horror! For some reason I can't guess the mortar is not perished by your chanting, nor do the slates fall when you wave the sapling sticks. (He goes towards her) As for windows, none, or fingernails in width. Stuff light. Stuff furnishings! (p. 23.)*

In so far as the castle connotes male sexuality, it is a sexuality erected in defiance of the female, violent, hard and comfortless. Krak had stated in Scene 2 that the castle was not a 'house' — meaning not a domestic place where the masculine and feminine live together in peace and reconciliation. On the other hand, Stucley is exerting his power to insist on the **appearances** of domestic harmony:

> STUCLEY: ... *YOU DISCUSS THINGS LIKE A PROPER WIFE! (Pause) Terrible impertinence. (pp. 23–24.)*

Stucley rushes off to hasten the building work leaving Ann with the newly ordained Nailer who is mumbling prayers in a corner with the tool bag/mitre on his head. When she tries to remonstrate with him, he vents his detestation of the women's never-ending discussions.

> *ANN: Reg, there is a tool bag on your head. (Pause. He regards her with contempt)*
> *NAILER: Oh, you literal creature … It was a tool bag … it is no longer a tool bag, it is a badge … IF YOU KNEW HOW I YEARNED FOR GOD!*
> *ANN: Which god? (Pause, then patiently)*
> *NAILER: The God which puts a stop to argument. The God who says, 'Thus I ordain it!' The God who puts His finger on the sin.*
> *ANN: Sin…?*
> *NAILER: WHY NOT SIN? (Pause. He gets up) And no more Reg. (He looks at her, goes out. A wind howls over the stage) (p. 25.)*

We have already seen how Hush desires his own subservience. This applies likewise to the more 'educated' and superficially liberal Nailer whose longing for God is a longing for dogma. What many seek from religion is simple certainty — literally an end to the argument — especially the argument about right and wrong. At the same time, Nailer's ordination means that he takes on a new, authoritative identity — *'no more Reg'*. The seductive challenge here is for Nailer to carry off his new identity in defiance of Ann insisting on his old one. In terms of seduction, he must be totally taken in by his own illusion. In this respect the transubstantiation of the tool bag is both symbolic and of the essence. As a man with a tool bag on his head, Nailer is an object of ridicule — as bishop in a mitre he is an object of veneration; it is an extreme test but, in his extremity, he succeeds triumphantly, marking yet another step in the onward march of the castle and the retreat of the women.

In Scene 5, the final scene of Act 1, Stucley appears, cavorting childishly in the wind. The castle has altered even the weather; he asks Krak to make it snow and when a flurry drifts across, he wrestles delightedly with the engineer. Suddenly Krak begins to strangle him and equally suddenly stops. Both men are shocked at the hatred Krak has revealed. The effect, however, sends both of them scurrying back to the building. After a pause, Skinner enters with Cant; it appears she has been using her witchcraft to make it snow — presumably to hinder the progress of the castle. The amount, however, initially at least, is negligible and she feels that she has lost the power: it is a moment for her of deep despair. There is a clear contrast here between the manipulative and coercive power of Krak's rational technology (*'the wind is trapped'*) and the seductive power of Skinner's witchcraft. (Typically in Barker's dramaturgy, there is no objective indication as to who or what has caused the snow.) At her request, Cant leaves her and, in the snow, she sees a nightmare vision of armoured figures swearing an oath of never-ending warfare and slaughter. This is another of Barker's male covens, bonded with ritual and secrecy. They dedicate themselves to an orgy of violence —

> — *until such tyme we have our aims all maken wholehearte and compleate!* (p. 26.)

What these '*aims*' might be is not mentioned and seems of little real importance; the '*aims*' are a means to the means which clearly amounts to an infatuation with atrocity:

> ROLAND: ... *The flaming cow ran with its entrails hanging out —*
> BALDWIN: *I cut the dog in half —*
> THEOBALD: *One blow —*
> BALDWIN: *The dog in two halves went —*
> THEOBALD: *The head this way —*
> ROLAND: *Its entrails caught around a post —*
> REGINALD: *Double-headed axe went — (p. 27.)*

As their voices cease, Holiday, the builder, enters —

> HOLIDAY: *Yep? (He looks around) Somebody ask for me? (Pause) (p. 28.)*

— in rational terms possibly in response to Stucley's call earlier in the scene — irrationally Skinner calls him with her 'underneath' just as she earlier accused Ann of calling Stucley.

> HOLIDAY: ... *(He is about to go, then, looking around him) I saw your arse... (Pause) Excuse me, but I saw your arse — you showed your arse and I — they say you don't like men — which is to do surely, with — who you 'ad to do with, surely ... (Pause) Anyway, I saw your arse... (He turns, despairingly, to go)*
> SKINNER: *All right.*
> HOLIDAY: *(stops) What — you —*
> SKINNER: *All right...*
> *(The walls rise to reveal the interior of a keep. Black out.) (p. 28.)*

In spite of its brevity and relatively undramatic nature, this is a seduction of crucial importance. Holiday has paradoxically found seduction in Skinner's gesture of contempt. He is well aware of the consciously intended meaning of the gesture but deliberately tries to subvert that by using it to establish a kind of intimacy between them. Skinner realises this but seizes the opportunity to kill the builder: in this world now dominated by reason, sexuality is the only natural magic left. It is significant that the sexuality in question is soulless and instrumental (Skinner claims later that the builder talked of *'mutual pleasure'*.) This 'dirty' quality is emphasised by Holiday's secretive approach — *'looking around him'*. The seduction also signals, as the final stage directions of the act indicate, a move into the interior of the castle.

Act 2 begins with Krak, in a soliloquy, describing the progress of the castle. It appears that Stucley is demanding more and more fortifications which, in a way, are logical extensions of each other. The process has clearly run away with Krak who has tried to persuade Stucley that he is secure enough already behind three walls.

> KRAK: ... *A fifth wall I predict will be necessary, and a sixth essential, to protect the fifth, necessitating the erection of twelve flanking towers. The castle is by definition, not definitive... (p. 29.)*

This mushrooming of the castle suggests that the original 'definitive' and exact creation has taken on a 'life' of its own which involves a constant and 'organic' process of reshaping — a process which is both escalatory and vertiginous. And all this is to confront an enemy who has not yet but *'cannot fail to materialize'*.

This is immediately followed by the hue and cry over Holiday's death which, it is quickly established, is a case of *'woman murder'*. Stucley's first concern is to complete the castle and he gives Holiday's job to his assistant, Brian.

> STUCLEY: WHO WILL TRANSLATE MY BLUEPRINTS NOW! (ANN *enters.* STUCLEY *turns on her) Who did this, you! Oh, her mask of kindness goes all scornful at the thought — what, me? (He swings on* BRIAN) YOU DO THE JOB! (And to ANN) *And such a crease of womanly dismay spreads down her jaw, and dignified long nose tips slightly with her arrogance — what, me?* IT STOPS NOTHING, THIS. (pp. 29–30.)

It is important to note that Ann's continuing silent and disapproving presence is a significant factor in Stucley's world. He is infuriated by her passive defiance and assumes here that her response to the murder and her *'womanly dismay'* are hypocritical. He sees his most effective counterstrike as being the continuation of the castle but with the addition of a new wall:

> STUCLEY: *Listen, I think morality is also bricks, the fifth wall is the wall of morals, did you think I could leave that untouched? (p. 30.)*

Stucley's comments here foreshadow his enforcing of morality with the trial of Skinner in the following scene. As I suggested earlier, he is retreating into a woman-hating male cameraderie.

Ann is left alone with Krak and seduces him, overwhelming his resistance with an inexorable feminine power:

> ANN: *Gravity. Parabolas. Equations. The first man's dead. Gravity. Parabolas. Equations. Are you glad? (KRAK does not move) Say yes. Because you are. That's why you're here. Grey head. Badger gnawed about the ears and eyes down, bitten old survivor of the slaughter, loosing off your wisdom when you think yourself alone, I know, I do know, grandfather of slain children, aping the advisor, aping the confidant, but actually, but actually, I do know badger-head, you want us dead. And not dead simply, but torn, parted, spiked on the oaks, limbs between the acorns, a real rucking of the favoured landscape, the peace when you came here made your heart knot with anger, I know, the castle is the magnet of extermination, it is not a house, is it, the castle is not a house... (Pause) I am so drawn to you I feel sick. (Pause) The man who suffers. The man who's lost. Success appalls me but pain I love. Your grey misery excites me. Can you stand a woman who talks of her cunt? I am all enlarged for you... (He stares at her) Now you humiliate me. By silence. I am not humiliated. (Pause) (p. 30.)*

Firstly, she confronts Krak with his secret purpose and his reasons for that purpose. After the pause, she states her intense attraction very directly. As is usual in seduction, it is not his strength but his weakness and hopeless misery which draws her. In stating her sexual attraction in this very direct way she gives him the opportunity of humiliating her: he attempts to shame her by staring silently. By stating his intention, thereby exposing the tactic, and deliberately refusing the shame, she redoubles the pressure on him. This is a familiar seductive tactic which I have already discussed with reference to numerous other Barker characters. Krak decides he has no alternative but to confront the issue:

> KRAK: *They cut off my mother's head. She was senile and complaining. They dismembered my wife, whom I saw little of. And my daughter, with a glancing blow, spilled all her brains, as a clumsy man sends the drink flying off the table. And her I did not give all the attention that I might. I try to be truthful. I hate exaggeration. I hate the cultivated emotion. (Pause) And you say, come under my skirt. Under my skirt, oblivion and compensation, shoot your anger in my bowel, CUNT ALSO IS A DUNGEON! (Pause)*
> ANN: *Enthralling shout... (Pause, then he suddenly laughs) And laugh, for that matter... (Pause, then he turns to leave) I mean, don't tell me it is virgins that you want, the unmarked flesh, untrodden map of girlhood, the look of fear and unhinged legs of — (He returns, slaps her face into silence. Pause) You have made my nose bleed... (p. 30.)*

When he describes the various fates of his family, Krak appears to be trying to put his emotions into perspective by distancing himself from them: he is being objective and rational — remaining in control. The seductive ingredient of these qualifications, however, is guilt; this is particularly clear when he talks of his neglected daughter. When he turns savagely on Ann with '*CUNT ALSO IS A DUNGEON*', it is because he sees no possibility of salvation for himself in what she is offering. Instead of addressing his accusation, she rejoices in his emotional release. He tries to counter this by releasing his intensity in laughter and simultaneously signalling contempt: again, this is unprecedented for him (Ann commented earlier that he never smiled). As a rebuff it fails. Finally, he tries to escape by walking out but she taunts him into returning and slapping her — a loss of self-control. In a metaphorical sense, it is almost as if she systematically breaches each of the walls he refers to at the beginning of the scene.

It is worth commenting, at this point, on Krak's name which in the historical context of the Crusades suggests the famous castle, Krak des Chevaliers. 'Krak' or 'kerak' is the Levantine Arabic word for 'fortress'. So Krak too is the castle both by name and by nature in that he exists behind an elaborate system of defences. Barker is also evoking the English homophone — 'crack'; appropriately, the first phrase cited in connection with this word in the Concise Oxford Dictionary is 'crack of doom'; even more significant in the context of the play is the slang use of the word to mean 'cunt' (see Partridge). Krak's obsessive drawing of fortifications becomes obsessive drawing of 'cunt' later in the play.

Another significant link connects Krak with Pain in *Crimes in Hot Countries*; T.E. Pain is Barker's version of Lawrence of Arabia. Like Krak, Pain is very consciously 'the genius', the man of massive intellectual power; like Krak, he is located 'in exile' — not merely in the 'hot country' but in the cultural desert of the 'other ranks' of the British Army, casting his perfectly phrased pearls before swinish squaddies; like Krak, he enjoys a privileged if ambiguous relationship with authority which is mesmerised by his seductive charisma; on another level, the violent and thuggish Music's attraction to Pain's intellectual sophistication parallels Batter's fascination with Krak. Both geniuses have a passion for military strategy and classical logic. Barker has reversed the Lawrence situation in the case of Krak; instead of an Englishman devising Arab military strategy in Arabia, an Arab devises English military strategy in England. The 'historical' Lawrence was a devotee of Medieval castles, travelling inter 1905–1910 thousands of miles on foot and by bicycle in Britain, France, Syria and Palestine to visit notable sites. The fruit of these investigations was the thesis he submitted for his degree at Oxford, later published under the title '*Crusader Castles*' (1936).[11] In it, he enthuses over Krak des Chevaliers as *'perhaps the best preserved and most wholly admirable castle in the world'*.[12] A notable feature of this fortress is its great south wall, known to Arab historians as 'the mountain', which, towards its base, eschews the vertical in favour of a steep slope — a feature described in architectural parlance as a 'batter'. Of this, Lawrence says:

The reason for making the wall with so great a batter and such thickness — nearly 80 feet — is a little hard to find. Against an earthquake it would be useful perhaps, though no part of Crac has been damaged by one: the castle stands on rock, so mining was not greatly to be feared: and half the thickness would have been secure against any ram that ever was imagined.[13]

Krak des Chevaliers provides not only the name — Batter — but also the enigma of a strength massively in excess of any conceivable demands which might be made upon it — bringing to mind Stucley's *'unknown enemy ... who does not exist yet but who cannot fail to materialize.'* (p. 29.) Lawrence also remarks on the entry to Krak which is via a vaulted passageway described as *'almost dark'*, *'dark'*, *'steeply ascending'* and *'most confusing'*. When Ann proposes to Krak that they leave the castle, she says:

It is you that needs to be born. I will be your midwife. Through the darkness, down the black canal — (p. 35.)

comprising yet another symbolic connection between the castle's architecture and the human body. Finally, there is the 'historical' Lawrence himself — dazzling seducer of establishment luminaries, the enigmatic 'genius' with iron self-control and tortured sexuality — but also the supreme bluffer, poseur, charlatan and betrayer who serves to remind us that Krak, although he claims to *'hate the cultivated emotion'*, is certainly not beyond cultivating appearances: the all-rational military 'genius', whom Stucley refers to as *'the Great Amazer'*, is also a performance.

Act 2 Scene 2 is a trial scene. Barker has always been particularly adept at satirising the protocols and etiquettes of groups who consider themselves social elites — especially, as is usually the case, when these comprise an all-male preserve. The scene begins with the arrival of the two prosecutors. Nailer puts the prosecution case in a manner which is erudite, objective, balanced and apparently motivated by a selfless concern for the general good. The informal chat the two have before formal proceedings begin, however, subverts completely their 'official' performance:

NAILER: *Thank you for coming.*
POOL: *Thank you for asking me.*
NAILER: *The rigours of travel.*
POOL: *Not to be undertaken lightly.*
NAILER: *No, indeed. Indeed, no. His trousers were down.*
POOL: *So I gather.*
NAILER: *I do think —*
POOL: *The absolute limit.*
NAILER: *And misuse of love.*

> POOL: *Make that your angle.*
> NAILER: *I will do.*
> POOL: *The trust which resides in the moment of —*
> NAILER: *Etcetera-*
> POOL: *Most cruelly abused. Make that your angle.*
> NAILER: *Thank you, I will.*
> POOL: *Fucking bitches when your goolies are out…*
> NAILER: *(To the court) A man proffers union — albeit…. (pp. 30–31.)*

It can be seen here how formal pleasantries rapidly lead on through a process of hints to expressions of male solidarity in outrage and, finally, deep misogyny. The mask of Nailer's 'rhetoric' is exposed even before it is proposed. What is 'different' about this trial is that Skinner's crime is not simply murder (in the world of the castle, violent death does not per se excite moral outrage), but *'woman murder'*. Once Nailer starts his peroration. Barker intercuts this with a speech from Skinner which is addressed not to the court but to Ann; in terms of staging this needs to be produced in a stylised manner to suggest the two speeches are in fact going on simultaneously (there is no communication whatsoever between defendant and prosecutor — they exist on different planes). Nailer's case is that in offering sexual intercourse, the man lays aside *'all those defences which the male by nature transports in his demeanour.'*

> NAILER: *A crime therefore, not against an individual — not against a single man most cruelly deceived… but against that universal trust, that universally upheld convention lying at the heart of all sexual relations…. And thereby threatening not only the security of that most intimate love which God endowed man with… for peace and relief but… the very act of procreation itself…. (p. 31.)*

The siege mentality of the castle serves to generate hysterical fears about any remaining areas of potential vulnerability or insecurity. The work of the court therefore seeks to establish and encase the sexual relation 'within a secure framework of law.' External law being — as I have argued — fundamental to the control-based world of rationality — as opposed to the immanent rule of seduction. The contemporary resonances of this process are, perhaps, too obvious to require any specific comment.

Dramatically the most powerful aspect of the scene is contributed by Skinner. She is brought into the court having been hideously tortured so that her utterances have the appearances of abjection and at times madness. Her concern is to speak to Ann and to express her anger:

> SKINNER: *ANN!…ANN!…WHERE ARE YOU, YOU BITCH — no, mustn't swear —*
> *(p. 31.)*

4. The trial of Skinner. *The Castle*, Act II, Scene 2.

The physical memory of the torture she has suffered, causes her to check her outbursts and apologise abjectly: as she says of her tormenters:

> — *beg pardon* — *I have this* — *tone which* — *thanks to your expertise is mollified a little* —
> (p. 32.)

She attributes her anger to the unaccustomed exposure to daylight and tries desperately to reassure all that she is genuinely 'reformed':

> SKINNER: *I am not ill-tempered as a matter of fact, I don't know where that idea's come from that I* — *and anyway I know you hate it, loudness and shouting, you do, such delicate emotions and I* — THEY HAVE DONE AWFUL THINGS TO ME DOWN THERE — *do my best to be* — *to be contained* — *that way you have, you* — THERE IS A ROOM DOWN THERE AND THEY DID TERRIBLE THINGS TO ME — *I mean my cunt which had been so* — *which we had made so* — THANKS TO YOU WAS DEAD — *so it wasn't the abuse it might have been, the abuse they would have liked it to be had it been a living thing, were it the sacred and beautiful thing we had found it out to be and* — *am I going on, I do go on* — *are you* — *so thank you I hated it and the more they hurt it the better I* — *I was actually gratified, believe it or not, yes, gratified* — (p. 31.)

The words in capitals indicate breaches in Skinner's self-control and should be blurted — almost involuntarily. Barker deliberately seeks to make the words 'DOWN THERE' ambiguous, intending them to signify both dungeon and cunt. This follows through consistently the symbolic theme of equating the land with the female body. The dungeon is, conventionally, where the edifice of the castle penetrates the land — underground. The most significant statement, however, is Skinner's assertion that she willed the torture of her sexual organs; she wanted her cunt to suffer because Ann had betrayed their love ('*my cunt which...THANKS TO YOU WAS DEAD*'). This is another example of a crucial seductive reversal, an acceptance and willing of calamity which parallels Stucley's acceptance of the lashes of fate administered to him by a cruel and sadistic deity.

The central thematic of this scene is of a tortured sexuality — in the widest possible sense of that phrase. Skinner's words referring to her own sufferings are clearly relevant to the institutionalised misogyny of patriarchal society:

> *They think of everything* — *they do* — *imaginations* — *you should see the* — INVENTION DOWN THERE — *makes you gasp the length of their hatred* — *the uncoiled length of hatred* — (p. 32.)

Peering round the court, Skinner is unable to see Ann and asks for a stool to sit on. When one is brought, she leaps back from it expecting a trap, then in complete contradiction to her alarm, she sinks wearily onto it — as if she didn't care whether it bit her or not; this kind of sudden change of attitude is typical of her fragmented personality in this scene.

If Skinner seems here remote and disconnected from the court, Stucley is even more so:

> STUCLEY: ...Having hewn away two hills to make us safe, having knifed the landscape to preserve us we find — horror of horrors — THE WORST WITHIN. (Pause, he looks at all of them) I find that a blow, I do, I who have reeled under so many blows find that — a blow. Who can you trust? TRUST! (He shrieks at them, the word is a thing butted at them) I say in friendship, I say in comradeship, I say without malice YOU ARE ALL TRAITORS! (p. 32.)

Stucley's intensifying paranoia in this scene clearly marks another stage in the escalating process of the castle: he goes on to insist on all the repressive measures of a police state. Nailer shows that he understands his role as ideologist:

> STUCLEY: ...I have changed my view of God. I no longer regard Him as an evil deity, that was excessive, evil, no. He's mad. It is only by recognizing God is mad that we can satisfactorily explain the random nature of — you say, you are the theologian.
> NAILER: It appears to us He was not always mad —
> STUCLEY: Not always, no —
> NAILER: But became so, driven to insanity by the failure and contradiction of His works —
> STUCLEY: I understand Him! (p. 32–33.)

Stucley requires a deity fabricated in his own image. As a tyrant, giving ear only to what he wants to hear, he presumably surrounds himself with people like Nailer. From this scene on, his presence conveys a sinister remoteness which most of us are familiar with only from witnessing on television the grotesque charades of third world dictators. Particularly bizarre and embarrassing are his reference in open court to his sexual incontinence:

> STUCLEY: ... I sleep alone in sheets grey with tossing, I cannot keep a white sheet white, do you find this? Grey by the morning. Does anyone find this? The launderers are frantic.
> BATTER: Yes.
> STUCLEY: You do? What is it?
> BATTER: I don't know... it could be... I don't know...
> STUCLEY: Why grey, I wonder? (p. 33.)

While it is necessary to express agreement with him, Batter finds it impossible to state the obvious. Like Skinner, Stucley presents another aspect of tortured sexuality. Barker also makes Stucley express himself in a manner similar to Skinner, suddenly blurting out statements which appear involuntarily to voice deep-seated fears, intuitions and repressions:

STUCLEY: THEY ARE BUILDING A CASTLE OVER THE HILL AND IT'S BIGGER THAN THIS. (Pause) Given God is now a lunatic, I think, sadly, we are near to the Apocalypse... (p. 33.)

The first of these sentences should sound almost as if spoken by another person; when Stucley reverts to 'character' to speak the second sentence, it should be performed as if the first sentence hadn't been uttered. His intuition about the other castle — it is at this stage pure intuition, though confirmed in the following scene — together with his thoughts on the Apocalypse strongly suggest that he is in the grip of a powerful death wish.

Suddenly Skinner sees Ann and leaps to her feet:

SKINNER: WHAT HAVE YOU DONE TO YOUR HAIR? (Pause) It's plaited in a funny way, what have you — IT'S VILE. (Pause) Well, no, it's not, it's pretty, vile and pretty at the same time, DID YOU TAKE HIM IN YOUR MOUTH, I MUST KNOW. (p. 33.)

It will be recalled that Skinner had said previously that the castle would affect everything — even the way Ann plaited her hair; she is particularly shocked because her former lover's appearance strikes her as being intended to please someone else. A violent spasm of jealousy gives way after a pause to melancholy reflection:

SKINNER: ... This floor, laid over flowers we once laid on, this cruel floor will become the site of giggling picnics, clots of children wandering with music in their ears and not one will think, not one, A WOMAN WRITHED HERE ONCE. The problem is to divest yourself of temporality, is that what you do? (She looks at NAILER) I gave up, and longed to die, and yet I did not die. That all life should be bound up in one randomly encountered individual defies the dumb will of the flesh clamouring for continuation, life would not have it! I hate you, do you know why, because you prove to me that nothing is, nothing at all is, THE THING WITHOUT WHICH NOTHING ELSE IS POSSIBLE. (p. 33.)

Skinner said in Act 1 Scene 3 that it was *'the pain of witches to see to the very end of things'*; here, she sees beyond the physical end of the castle to the contemporary world with its indifference to her struggles; the word 'writhed' is deliberately ambiguous implying both sexual love and torture. Her comment about temporality indicates that she recognises this awareness of time is precisely the source of her pain. Nailer, whom she addresses here, seems to have no difficulty in consigning to oblivion all previous commitments and professions of faith in the interests of physical survival — *'the dumb will of the flesh clamouring for continuation'*. She sees that her commitment to Ann (*'one randomly encountered individual'* is opposed by life itself — which is why she wanted to die. Life itself, however, would not let her die. She hates both Ann and life because they have proved to her that *'the thing without which nothing else is possible'* — love — does not exist. In banal terms, she is disillusioned. Her language indicates that she has succumbed to the world of banality, of rationalism: Ann is referred to as *'one randomly encountered individual'* but the concept of 'the random' is essentially rational; in seduction, it doesn't exist because everything is destiny. In Act 1 Scene 3, Krak stated:

> KRAK: ...*The whole of life serves to remind us that we exist among inert banality. (p. 16.)*

Skinner who insisted that there was no separate *'love life'*, that *'the colour of the love stains everything'*, that one did not step from one life to the other — *'banality to love, love to banality' (p. 19.)*, now lives *'amongst inert banality'*.

Skinner's performance here is based on the confident assumption that she is about to be executed — which is what she wants; death will at least provide the oblivion she seeks. However, in a fit of bravado, she dismisses the right of the court and challenges Stucley to pass sentence — on the grounds that only those who have suffered like herself should have this prerogative. In so doing, she underestimates his cruelty. What Stucley had found so irresistibly seductive about his deity was not death, as Skinner earlier states, but *'his grasp of pian and pressure' (p. 9.)*. He takes up Skinner's challenge and sentences her to the embrace of the rotting corpse of her victim:

> STUCLEY: *Tie her to the body of her victim. (Pause)*
> SKINNER: *Tie her to —*
> STUCLEY: *And turn her loose. (p. 33.)*

She is horrified.

Scene 3 begins with massive explosions and panic. Krak tells Stucley that there is — in actual fact — another castle in the East:

> KRAK: *You knew, and I knew, there could not be only this one, but this one would breed others. And there is one. Called the Fortress.*
> STUCLEY: *Bigger than this...*
> KRAK: *Bigger. Three times the towers and polygonal. With ravelins beyond a double ditch, which I never thought of ... (STUCLEY stares for a moment in disbelief)*
> STUCLEY: *Everything I fear, it comes to pass. Everything I imagine is vindicated. Awful talent I possess. DON'T I HAVE AN AWFUL TALENT? TALENT? (p. 34.)*

Barker's writing demonstrates very clearly how Stucley's death-wish works. It is significant that his line — *'Bigger than this ...'* — is not a question; by positing the other castle in his imgination, ultimately he conjures it into

5.　'There is one…' *The Castle*, Act II, Scene 3.

reality. He is seduced by the power of his capacity to envisage catastrophe, his intuitive comprehension of a cruel fate. He orders massive increases in the fortifications of the castle, — increases which confound Krak. After a fourth boom, Stucley demands to know what the noise is:

> KRAK: *The coming of the English desert… (Pause)*
> STUCLEY: *Yes…*
> NAILER: *Almighty! Almighty!*
> STUCLEY: *Yes…*
> NAILER: *Oh, Almighty, Oh, Almighty…!*
> STUCLEY: *Extinction of the worthless, the obliteration of the melancholy crawl from the puddle to the puddle, from the puddle of the maternal belly to the puddle of the old man's involuntary bladder… Good… and they make such a fuss of murder… NOT ME THOUGH.* (p. 34.)

Stucley assents to universal destruction, the extinction of a life which is worthless. His final words reassert his rigorous self-control, his stoicism and his sense of superiority. The events of this scene serve to intensify the doom-laden atmosphere and sense of looming catastrophe.

The others all depart leaving Krak who reflects uneasily on the new castle or perhaps rather on the mind of its designer — an enigma to him. Ann enters, pregnant, and proposes that they leave together:

> ANN: *We find a rock.*
> KRAK: *Stink of death to English woods. Hips on the fences. Flies a noisy garment on the entrail in the bracken.*
> ANN: *I have your child in here.*
> KRAK: *The trooper boots the bud open and sends my — (Pause) Said my, then… (Pause. He smiles) Error.* (p. 35.)

The present situation seems to represent the fulfilment of Krak's secret purpose — the total destruction of his captors and their land. Here he attempts to cling to this strategy in the face of Ann insisting that he cannot simply divorce himself from life in the way that Stucley has; he is involved through his child. Because his present life as birthed by Batter is in fact dedicated to death, she offers herself as midwife for yet another birth. He tells her (and here there is a clear parallel with nuclear warfare) that there is no refuge or escape from the death-engines of the castle. Ann turns on him with what is her first truly violent outburst:

> ANN: *ALL RIGHT, WISDOM! ALL RIGHT, LOGIC! (Pause) I have a child in here, stone deaf to argument, floats in water, all pessimism filtered, lucky infant spared compelling reasons why it should acquiesce in death. (She turns to go)*
> KRAK: *IS THERE ANY MAN YOU HAVE NOT COPULATED WITH? (She stops) I wonder…* (p. 35.)

What Ann is roused to anger by is the spiritual and ideological climate of acceptance of death, the malaise and miasma which dominate the castle; also, as I have remarked already, she has always believed in the possibility of passing on — of 'otherness' — now she finds herself trapped. As she turns to go, Krak attempts to distance himself from her and the child. I think that the stage direction here — *She stops* — is particularly important, suggesting that his comment has wounded her deeply. His follow-up — '*I wonder...*' — indicates that he realises this and is, in a clumsy way, an attempt to retract.

Before she can leave, however, Skinner enters with the corpse of Holiday strapped to her front, an object of contempt and abuse. The stage directions say she is '*a grotesque parody of pregnancy*' and as such she confronts the pregnant Ann. Her first statements all concern the practicalities of coping with her condition which she ironically likens to pregnancy — '*much morning sickness all times of the day*'. Her condition has brought about two horrific discoveries: firstly, she has gotten used it and in fact quite accepts it (when Ann suggests that she go elsewhere to '*find peace and rub the thing off you*', she refuses — '*Yes to punishment. Yes to blows.*') Secondly, she has discovered she can live without others and seems to take a certain pride in the uniqueness of her state. Ann weeps in despair but Krak stares fixedly at Skinner throughout the scene in much the same way as he stared at the hill in Act 1, building a dramatic tension. Ann's distress is, at least in part, because she feels she is responsible for Skinner's plight — a notion Skinner herself derides, mockingly warning Krak:

> SKINNER: *...Careful! She's after your suicide! Hanging off the battlements for love! The corpse erect! Through her thin smile the knowledge even in death she got you up! (Mimicking) Did I do this? (She turns to ANN) This is my place, more stones the better and pisspans, pour on! You and your reproductive satisfactions, your breasts and your lactation, dresses forever soddened at the tit, IT DID GET ON MY WICK A BIT, envy of course, envy, envy, envy of course. I belong here. I am the castle also.*
> ANN: *You do suck your hatreds. You do — suck — so. And he — also sucks his. (p. 36.)*

Skinner's attitude to Ann manifests a pattern fairly similar to Stucley's: passionate love followed by violent and anguished hatred, followed by a settled hatred as expressed here; it will be recalled that Stucley similarly mimicked and sneered at his wife's femininity. Skinner sees Ann here as deliberately thirsting for the anguish and suffering she leaves in her wake, — even though she pretends that it distresses her. Skinner also admits her envy of Ann's fertility — an envy which apparently was always there: her final words here indicate that she feels it is because of this envy that she '*belongs*' — she too is the castle. Ann's comment points out how Skinner and Krak and Stucley are comparable in feeding off negative emotions — a few lines further on she specifies pessimism and fear. Her words are illustrated immediately when a group of hooded prisoners shuffle in; Skinner gleefully directs them to the dungeon and mockingly anticipates what is in store for them. Batter, who is conducting them, confirms her status as an accepted part of castle life by greeting her in a familiar and almost friendly fashion:

> BATTER: *English summer…*
> SKINNER: *Fuckin' 'ell…*
> BATTER: *(as he passes). Take care…*
> SKINNER: *Will do… (p. 37.)*

Ann, unable to contemplate this, has already fled, so when Batter and the prisoners file out, the silent and staring Krak is left alone with Skinner who unconcernedly starts to eat an apple.

To Skinner's amazement, Krak suddenly kneels at her feet:

> KRAK: *The Book of Cunt. (Pause)*
> SKINNER: *What book is that?*
> KRAK: *The Book of Cunt says all men can be saved. (p. 37.)*

Beginning to doubt the value of science with which he has identified himself, he sees in Skinner an alternative to the beliefs he confidently proclaimed. It will be recalled that she had confronted him in Act 1 Scene 2 draped in flowers and ordered him to contemplate the *'superior geometry'* of a flower; then, he completely ignored her. What draws him to nature, however, is not the flower but cunt:

> KRAK: *Where's cunt's geometry? The thing has got no angles! And no measure, neither width nor depth, how can you trust what has no measurements? Don't tell them I came here… (p. 37.)*

Skinner seduces Krak intellectually; he sees her essentially as an enigmatic source of female wisdom (the symbolism of the apple-eating strongly suggests this): whereas before, her conscious struggle to move him did nothing, he is seduced now by her self-possession and indifference. Krak's 'confession' to Skinner shows that he is in a state of confusion. Ann has sexually seduced him and in that seduction he finds the promise of salvation:

> KRAK: *… She pulled me down. I did not pull her. She pulled me. In the shadow of the turret, in the apex of the angle with the wall, in the slender crack of thirty-nine degrees, she, using the ledge to fix her heels, levered her parts over me. Shoes fell, drawers fell, drowned argument in her spreading underneath… (Pause) European woman with her passion for old men, wants to drown their history in her bowel…! (Pause)*

SKINNER: Scares you… (p. 37.)

Krak's description of Ann's actions here with the references to his fortifications is intended to suggest the breaching of the castle: she takes him by force. What had attracted Ann to him was his pain, his history; this she absorbs into her body, providing him with oblivion and peace. Krak is compulsively drawn to questioning Skinner here because she had known Ann as a lover. The possibility of salvation, however, lies in cunt which has no fixed geometrical properties, — as such it cannot be controlled in the way that rational constructs can. Krak is terrified at the possibility of his fate being beyond his control. His repeated plea — *'Don't tell them I came here'* — suggests that commerce with Skinner is forbidden in spite of the fact that her presence is tolerated. The arrival of Cant and Hush with food for her indicates that she is becoming a focus of dissent within the castle; her previous opposition together with her apparent martyrdom will confer an aura of deity upon her. As Harriet Walter, who played Skinner in the first RSC production of the play in 1985, says:

> …*the only time she wins back support is when she is considered a figure who is emptied, who has conquered pain and is above and beyond desire and therefore a political totem, the perfect leader. She attracts the villagers with their thought of that personal vacuum…*[14]

The realisation nevertheless comes as a shock to Skinner:

> *SKINNER: Oh, God, Oh, Nature, I AM GOING TO BE WORSHIPPED. (p. 37.)*

These words suggest she sees this as yet another trick played by a cruel and ironic fate: she has just accommodated herself to total abjection; she is not actually being worshipped as yet but she suddenly intuits the next cards she will be dealt because, like Stucley, she understands and can anticipate the mind of God.

In Scene 4, Stucley confronts Krak with an accusation of treachery, claiming that he has personally witnessed him trading drawings with the engineer of the Fortress. Krak is apparently unimpressed by this; his pride in his creation, which in Act 1 Scene 2 he claimed could not be destroyed, has been shattered:

> *KRAK: Gave him all my drawings. And got all his. They are experimenting with a substance that can bring down walls without getting beneath them. Everything before this weapon will be obsolete. This, for example is entirely redundant as a convincing method of defence —* (p. 39.)

6. 'Don't draw cunt, I'm talking…' *The Castle*, Act II, Scene 4.

In broad historical terms this can be seen to correspond to the redundancy of vertical fortification in the face of massive advances in firepower. In terms of the three classic elements of military strategy — armour, firepower and mobility, the castle represented the zenith of armour. Defence from firepower thereafter was sought by digging down into the earth – as in trench warfare. In a sense, however, there was a conceptual resurgence of the castle in Reagan's 'Star Wars' project with its aim of providing a totally secure defence umbrella against nuclear attack.

Krak has lost interest in military architecture and is obsessively drawing cunt — *'in 27 versions'*. It is interesting to note the element if unlikely continuity between castle and cunt in this respect. The former had started life as a single sharply and geometrically definitive drawing; gradually as more walls and towers were added, Krak was forced to admit that the definition was lost — *'The castle is by definition, not definitive…'*. Now he pours out drawing after drawing in an attempt to define the indefinite. (And here there is a parallel with another 'genius' whose name is linked to military architecture — Leonardo Da Vinci.) As was the case with Ann, in spite of his outrage, it is clear that Stucley is prepared to overlook or turn a blind eye to any treachery, provided that Krak humours him and they carry on with the game:

> STUCLEY: *DON'T DRAW CUNT. I'M TALKING!* (Pause) *This is a crisis, isn't it? Is it, or isn't it? You sit there — you have always been so — had this — manner of stillness — most becoming but also sinister — dignity but also malevolence — easy superiority of the captive intellect — IS THAT MY WIFE'S BITS — I wouldn't know them — what man would — I know, you see — I am aware — I do know everything — I do — I think you have done this all to spite me — correct me if I'm wrong —*
> KRAK: *Spite —*
> STUCLEY: *Spite me, yes —*
> KRAK: *Spite? I do not think the word — unless my English fails me — is quite sufficient to contain the volume of the sentiment…* (p. 38.)

The relationship between Krak and Stucley has also been a seductive duel — a game of challenging each other by constantly escalating the castle — now one has demanded staggering additional defences, now the other; latterly Krak, who has lost his positive, creative fascination with the castle, has challenged Stucley by his relationship with Ann and by his blatant treachery: he is pushing the limits of Stucley's dependence on the castle and on himself. Stucley, for his part, is prepared to use his weakness and dependence to seduce Krak — *'This is a crisis, isn't it?* Even when the moment of confrontation is forced upon him and he voices the ultimate unspeakable secret — that Krak had intended the castle to destroy him (which he knows and Krak knows he knows and he knows Krak knows he knows etc.) — he plays his weakness in the rider — *'correct me if I'm wrong-'*. Ann had accused Krak of *'aping the adviser, aping the confidant'*, the problem for Krak is how far he is seduced by his own role-playing — and by Stucley. This moment, for the latter, represents another catastrophe similar to his confrontation with Ann in Act 1 Scene 1. What amazes him is the magnitude of Krak's anger and the measure of his self-control:

> STUCLEY: *You blind draughtsman... all the madness in the immaculately ordered words... in the clean drawings... all the temper in the perfect curve... (He pretends to flinch) MIND YOUR FACES! DUCK HIS GUTS! INTELLECTUAL BURSTS! (p. 38.)*

He attempts to refuse Krak's 'spite' in the same way that Ann refused Krak's attempt to humiliate her:

> STUCLEY: *...But I am not spited. If you do not feel spited no amount of spite can hurt you, Christ was the same, NIGEL! (Pause) We burn people like this. Who give away our secrets. Burn them in a chair. Fry them, and the fat goes — human fat goes, spit...! Does — spit! (p. 39.)*

As he did with Skinner, Stucley seeks here to turn the tables on Krak by an act of malevolent imagination which takes his opponent's move and caps it, a seductive reversal: he will return Krak's 'spite' by physically transforming him into 'spit(e)'. While a desire to punish Krak might be deemed rational, the particular form it takes here is consonant only with the pure artifice of seduction.

At this point Ann enters and looks at them:

> ANN: *The ease of making children. The facility of numerousness. Plague, yes, but after the plague, the endless copulation of the immune. All these children, children everywhere and I thought, this one matters, alone of them this one matters because it came from love. But I thought wrongly. I thought wrongly. (Pause, She looks at KRAK) There is nowhere except where you are. Correct. Thank you. If it happens somewhere, it will happen everywhere. There is nowhere except where you are. Thank you for truth. (Pause. She kneels, pulls out a knife) Bring it down. All this. (She threatens her belly. Pause)*
> STUCLEY: *You won't. (Pause) You won't because you cannot. Your mind wants to, but you cannot, and you won't...*
> *(Pause. He holds out his hand for the knife. She plunges it into herself. A scream. The wall flies out. The exterior wall flies in. In a panic, SOLDIERS. Things falling.) (p. 39.)*

Ann's speech here should be considered in the light of Krak's sneer in the previous scene when he rejected her — *'IS THERE ANY MAN YOU HAVE NOT COPULATED WITH?'* as well as Skinner's and Stucley's jibes at her fertility. She is shattered by what she sees as her failure in love with Krak, and has decided to kill herself and her child. She has taken the logic of

7.   'Raining women. *The Castle*, Act II, Scene 5.

Krak's assertion that there is nowhere else and has intuited from this that '*If it happens somewhere, it will happen everywhere*'. Like Skinner and Stucley, she feels she has lost love but understands clearly that love is not possible in the life of the castle and no 'other' life is possible. The will to love can only triumph by willing the end of the life of the castle. There is also a sense here that her threat is a challenge to Krak (the stage directions say she looks at him); she pauses after saying '*I thought wrongly*', giving him the opportunity to disagree; she pauses when she kneels, when she threatens her belly and there are pauses during and after Stucley's lines; throughout all of these Krak refuses to intervene. The stage directions at the end of the scene suggest the cosmic repercussions of Ann's individual act. The castle remains but the action is flung outside; this is the first step in its demolition, in the sense that it no longer encompasses everything but is present now as an object.

In the '*haze of light*', we discover that the '*things falling*' are the bodies of pregnant women who are throwing themselves in vast numbers off the walls. Ann's death has proved as seductive as she perhaps intuited it would be and has been the catalyst which sparked off a suicide epidemic amongst the other women. This spectacular sequence shifting rapidly from Ann's suicide to the mass suicides outside the castle, parallels the sequence in Act 1 when Krak seduces Stucley with the plan and suddenly we are presented with its implementation. Nailer vainly threatens the women with judgement in the afterlife but finally orders the imprisonment and shackling of all those who are pregnant. Batter, who has already shown signs of impatience with Stucley as well as aimiability towards Skinner, doubtfully asks Cant's opinion:

> CANT: *We birth 'em, and you kill 'em. Can't be right we deliver for your slaughter. Cow mothers. Not an opinion. (p. 40.)*

A dazed Krak wanders among the bodies of the dead women, reflecting on his relationship with Ann:

> KRAK: *She undressed me… (They look at him) I lay there thinking… what is she… what does she… undressed me and… (Pause) What is the word?*
> BATTER: *Fucked?*
> KRAK: *Fucked! (He laughs, as never before) Fucked! (Pause) Went over me… the flesh… with such… inch by inch with such… (Pause) What is the word?*
> CANT: *Desire. (He stares at her, then throwing himself at her feet, tears open his shirt, exposing his flesh to her)*
> KRAK: *Show me. (p. 40.)*

He is still attempting to reduce his experience with Ann to a set of concepts, reproducible technology — an attitude which lies at the basis of much

8. Skinner with the skeleton.

contemporary thinking about sex: in fact the whole notion of a science of sexuality is inimical to seduction and desire. Krak insists on Cant attempting to demonstrate and replicate desire; she makes half-hearted efforts to touch him then runs out.

> *KRAK: Not it…*
> *CANT: Trying but I…*
> *KRAK: Not it!*
> *CANT: Can't just go —*
> *KRAK: NOT IT! NOT IT! (p. 40.)*

When Stucley enters and sees him, he immediately recognises his condition:

> *STUCLEY: Lost love…! Nothing, nothing like lost love… (He rests a hand on KRAK's bent head) And she was of such sympathy, such womanly wisdom I could not bring myself to take revenge, any man would, you say, yes, any man would! Not me, though…! (He draws KRAK's head to his side) And you, dear brother in lost love, I UNDERSTAND. (pp. 40–41.)*

Stucley can reconcile himself to Krak in their common grief. The engineer's desolation is the greater because Ann's final gesture has implicated him in her fate and won the duel for her: he called her bluff in the matter of her suicide. Krak's belated discovery of love parallels Ilona's in *The Power of The Dog*: as with Lvov's in *The Last Supper*, the manner of Ann's death has had the effect of imposing an inescapable obligation on those implicated in it.

Amidst the general atmosphere of catastrophic grief, Stucley announces that the new walls will be built low thereby preventing such fatalities. They all stare at him and, after a pause, Batter invites him to go for a walk with him. Stucley demurs but Batter soothes him like a child, reminding him of former triumphs in Jerusalem, eventually picking him up and carrying him out in his arms. Stucley no longer has any power to resist; his very substance seems to have vanished leaving only a thin husk. The only person to protest is Krak:

> *KRAK: (to the soldiers) His last walk. His last walk. (They ignore him) Listen, his last walk…! (p. 41.)*

His intervention serves to underline that fact that there is a bond between himself and Stucley; the latter is not merely the hated captor marked down for destruction. As a final gesture, Krak offers the soldiers his own head to be sliced through with an axe:

> *KRAK: … Slice it round the top and SSSSSSS the great stench of dead language SSSSSSS the great stench of dead elegance dead manners SSSSSSS articulation and explanation dead all dead YOU DON'T HOLD WOMEN PROPERLY IN BED. (p. 41.)*

At the outset of the play, Krak considered the brain he offers here to be that of a genius, priding himself on his intellectual sophistication; now he considers all that as *'dead'* — and not only dead but putrifying. Interestingly, his words here (*'language'*, *'elegance'*, *'manners'*, etc.) seem to refer to his seductive charisma rather than his scientific skills per se. The important thing is *'to hold women properly in bed.'* This sentence betrays his persistently rationalist turn of mind: he realises that the whole catastrophe of the castle concerns relations between men and women; however, the notion that there is a 'proper' way of approaching this is perhaps somewhat reductive and a continuation of the thinking he has just shown in his 'experiment' with Cant.

The final scene, again outside the walls, begins with Batter and Nailer approaching Skinner with the offer of a new church. By this time the body of Holiday is reduced to a skeleton.

> BATTER: *New church. Tell her.*
> NAILER: *The Holy Congregation of the Wise Womb. (p. 41.)*

With the removal of Stucley, Batter wishes to set up a new state; as he appears to be wise to Hume's maxim that all government is founded solely upon opinion (we have already seen him fishing for Cant's), he has had Nailer assemble a new thealogy(sic):

> NAILER:... *We acknowledge the uniquely female relationship with the origin of life, the irrational but superior consciousness located in-*
> SKINNER: *Sod wombs* — (p. 42.)

This is obviously a reaction against the male, rationalist culture of Stucley's regime. Skinner is disinclined to cooperate because she hates wombs; being barren herself, she envied and resented Ann's easy fertility. Additionally she sees no reason why she should help Batter:

> SKINNER: ... *I won't help you govern your state, bailiff made monarch by a stroke of the knife... (p. 42.)*

He reflects for a moment and then offers power directly to her. At first, ever-suspicious, she thinks they are joking or playing some cruel trick, but when she realises they are sincere, the effect is dramatic:

> SKINNER: ... *Wait a minute, wait, what's your — get me swelling, get me gloating, dangle it before her eyes — she blobs about the eyes, the eyes are vast and breath goes in and out, in-out, in-out, pant, pant, the bitch is hooked, the bitch is netted, running with the water of desire GIVE ME POWER WHAT FOR — (Pause) All right yes... (p. 42.)*

9.   'No, you govern it instead…' *The Castle*, Act I, Scene 6.

Skinner's self-description here is of a sexual excitement but what produces this is not the prospect of sex but the prospect of power. When Nailer throws the keys down, she pounces upon them and instantly demands vengeance for all her sufferings:

> SKINNER: … *Reconciliation and oblivion, NO! GREAT UGLY STICK OF TEMPER RATHER (She turns on her heel) Nobody say it's all because I'm barren! I have had children, I have done my labour side by side, and felt myself halved by her spasms, my floor fell out with hers and yes, I haemorrhaged (Pause. They stare at her. She goes to the wall, runs her hand over the stone) I can't be kind. How I have wanted to be kind. But lost all feeling for it… Why wasn't I killed? The best thing is to perish in the struggle… (She turns to BATTER and NAILER) No. (She tosses the keys down) I shall be too cruel… (p. 43.)*

What one has to account for here is Skinner's sudden change of heart: how she can renounce the power which excited her so violently. In Act 1 Scene 1, Skinner reminded Ann of the births she refers to here:

> SKINNER: *I helped your births… And washed you, and parted your hair. I never knew such intimacy, did you? Tell me, all this unity! (pp. 6–7.)*

In recalling the shared births, she touches upon the moment when she was closest to Ann — so close in empathising with her birth-pains, that she herself bled. The resurgence of this terrible and painful memory in Skinner who has apparently succeeded in obliterating love from her life, momentarily counteracts her lust for vengeance and she turns to the castle wall as if searching for a way through. After a moment she despairs of the effort, feeling that kindness is now beyond her. Harriet Walter, the actress who played Skinner in the first production of the play, said:

> …*she knows she still has embers burning inside her which, in the final scene, she does not want to have stirred up again. Right at her core is a connection between power and love; if love is killed, what use is power —*[15]

When she renounces power, a voice is heard from the wall:

> KRAK: *Got to.*
> SKINNER: *Who says?*
> KRAK: *Got to! (Pause. She looks around)*
> SKINNER: *Out the shadows, who thinks the only perfect circle is the cunt in birth… (KRAK emerges from a cleft in the wall)*
> KRAK: *Demolition needs a drawing too… (Pause)*
> SKINNER: *Demolition? What's that? (A roar as jets streak low. Out of the silence, SKINNER strains in recollection) There was no government… does anyone remember… there was none… there was none… there was none…! (p. 43.)*

For a moment it seems as if the wall itself is speaking or Skinner is being exhorted by a disembodied imperative. It is significant symbolically that she summons Krak out of the wall — as if the human faculty that created it is now to be used against it. His comment on demolition serves to confirm this. It also implies, however, that the removal of the castle needs to be planned — a matter of organisation — which is why he insists she takes power. Skinner's assertion that there was no government may be seen as countering Krak's characteristic reliance on reason and power. But as the jets emphasise the essential contemporaneity of the play, the final impression of them both struggling with the issue, is a positive one.

In this examination of *The Castle*, I have attempted to sketch an outline of what might be said to happen in the play. To do this it has been necessary to consider the texture of the symbolism and to set the play within a wider cultural context in order to illuminate some of the thinking which informs it. Having done this, however, I am aware of a range of different possibilities available to performers at any particular moment in the drama. A character expresses an attitude; who is to say what their intention is? The actor performs the lines but this performance is informed by reacting with sensitivity to a context of the other characters' performances. What makes any performance dramatic is the extent to which the action is 'live' and actors are making genuine choices on stages: Barker's plays allow them to do precisely this. I have taken speeches at face value which could be played as bluff. Take, for example, Ann's suicide: does she adhere simply and unswervingly to a course of action determined before she enters — as might perhaps be the impression formed on an initial reading of the script? Could it be the case that she enters without the slightest intention of killing herself, confident in her power to force a response from Krak — as well perhaps as from the other party to the castle 'duet' — Stucley, — that both men 'see through' the bluff, 'call' it and force upon her an escalation she had not intended? Do her own words, initiated as a performance intended to seduce others finally and fatally end by seducing her? To what extent does she take Stucley's words — *'You won't'* — as the final and most crushingly humiliating challenge? To what extent are they intended as such? Or does Ann consider them merely impotent bluster, being entirely fixed upon Krak's obdurate silence? To what extent is Krak bluffing indifference?

In the Royal Shakespeare Company's premiere of *The Castle* (The Pit. October 1985), Penny Downie played Ann:

> *This is what I learnt more than anything from the play, that the Stanislavski idea of working in a totally logical set of progressions — 'if she eats this for breakfast than obviously she will be like this at lunch' — the questions 'who am I, what is my process' are useless.*[16]

She views character as essentially unstable:

> *With Ann, you are a walking set of contradictions, which create your character. It's not logical, it's very, very dangerous. Unless you've got danger — which is sexual energy onstage, to me — you're depriving an audience. To me, the most important thing is a character's sexuality, and therefore the way they think, it's extraordinarily dangerous. Your character becomes the sum total of the contradictions within it — you are your contradictions, you're not your logic — because if you always know how you're going to react in any given situation, you may as well just telephone it in!*[17]

The stress she lays upon 'sexual energy' corresponds with the emphasis I have placed upon seduction which is of course most easily and obviously identified within the context of sexuality; Penny Downie also specifically refers to the element of risk and the possibility of illogical reversal (contradictions) — both of which have been discussed as integral to the processes of seduction. An important factor in the potency of seduction is the sense of an opening up of possibilities:

> *It's made me completely reassess how I play a part. It's difficult, because it is a matter of letting go all your preconceptions and logic and, once you've made some preliminary choices, going onstage every night open and blank to some extent.*[18]

Penny Downie does emphasise, however, that this openness is an informed openness where the actor has fully considered all the implications and possibilities available to their character: it is in no sense a plea for the retention of some sort of unsophisticated naivety:

> *Harriet Walter's greatness in the role of Skinner was I think something to do with the fact that she'd made a lot of choices, she'd done heaps of work, technically, emotionally, examining possibilities and all of this was 'on tap', but was, on each night, open — that's what makes it wonderfully clean.*[19]

This studiedly ontological approach to acting, the eschewing of conscious objectives — particularly the highly structured and prescriptive systems of the Royal Court 'clarity' school of Gaskill and Stafford Clark — makes possible Grotowski's demand for a performance which is not willed:

> *To act — that is to react — not to conduct the process but to refer it to personal experiences and to be conducted. The process must take us.*[20]

Seduction is interaction and the energy of seduction arises out of interaction; by clearing the mind in the way suggested here, the performer lays him/herself open to respond with maximum sensitivity to other performers and to the audience.

While it is not inaccurate to say that Barker's characters 'perform' themselves, it needs to be emphasised firstly that the most important 'performances' are duets — not solos, and secondly that performances are often undercut or, as Barker puts it, 'abolished' by others. In productions of his work, the most salient impression has often tended to be of actors performing their own speech acts rather than reacting to those of others and, because he endows all his characters with articulacy, this can make it appear as if they are permanently 'in control' — a collection of impenetrable pebbles rattling around within the structure of the play. The essential drama, however, as I have suggested, is where control is relinquished in seduction or lost altogether and the emotional interactive process needs to be brought out strongly by the actors. Whether one defines this as 'subtext' is a matter of semantics; what is involved, however, is a secret economy, a shifting web of pacts, challenges, betrayals and complicities. Both *Judith* and *The Castle* demonstrate this clearly. It is interesting that, in the case of the premiere production of *The Castle*, the actors had actively to resist the director's attempts to impose ideological 'messages' upon the theatrical text. Kath Rogers, who played Cant:

> Nick Hamm, the director, was terrified that the play would be thought anti-feminist. He spent weeks... trying to soften the women — he kept saying: the audience will go mad, they won't listen to you. He didn't want us to be hard, he didn't want us to be unsympathetic, and we had to insist on our weaknesses, our flaws .... He would have liked us to hang up baby clothes, add Greenham incidents. We kept saying no... by making too many parallels with Greenham, you trivialise the play...[21]

As directors, actors, academics or audiences, we none of us approach a drama with completely 'open' minds, allowing the work to 'speak' directly to us. We bring expectations, preconceptions, 'knowledge', a mountain of second-hand experience in terms of which Barker is often dismissed as incomprehensible or ideologically unsound. I believe that contemporary requirements and expectations from theatre have become extremely narrow and specialised, the 'function' of drama 'understood' in terms of crude communication theories. In a way, people 'know' too much and all knowledge can serve to conceal. If my study has relied heavily on the philosophical, then this is because a return to first principles helps to put knowledge in perspective and opens up the possibility of **not knowing** — as Barker says 'the pain of unknowing', 'The ecstasy of not knowing for once'.[22] This, in turn, makes possible exploration and discovery. Barker uses the interactive format of drama to re-pose the question of what it means to be human; 'freedom and obligation, will and decision', as Szondi put it.[23] I would suggest that the concept of seduction provides an apposite focus for those concerned with staging his work. For seduction is the art of the irrational. Not to purvey a doctrine of irrationality. But only the irrational can challenge Reason (the active virtue, not the abstraction) into being. Just as it is only the moral dilemma, the moral abyss, the moral vacuum, — which activates serious ethical reflection. Democracy, the political practice of freedom, atrophies not when people believe the 'wrong' things but when the capacity to reason has fallen into general desuetude. The irrational is the necessary Other of Reason without which it quickly falls into its 'proper' vice of self-communion.

NOTES

INTRODUCTION

1. Howard Davies. 'Stock–Take at the Warehouse' in *Platform* 2, Summer 1980. p. 16.
2. Ronald Hayman. Review of *Hang of the Gaol* in *Plays and Players*, February 1979.
3. W. Stephen Gilbert. Review of *Fair Slaughter* in *Plays and Players*, July 1977.
4. James Fenton. Review of *The Loud Boy's Life* in *The Sunday Times*, 2 March 1980.
5. Howard Barker. Interview with Simon Trussler and Malcolm Hay in *New Theatre Voices of the Seventies*, Eyre Methuen 1981. p. 187.
6. *Claw* in *Stripwell & Claw* by Howard Barker, John Calder 1977. p. 136.
7. Ibid. p. 137.
8. Ibid. pp. 142–3.
9. *New Theatre Voices of the Seventies.* pp. 189 — 190.
10. *Claw.* p. 217.
11. Ibid. pp. 226–7.
12. Ibid. pp. 227–8
13. Ibid. p. 230.
14. Howard Barker. Unpublished Interview with Charles Lamb, 23 April 1987. Appendix to Doctoral Thesis *Irrational Theatre* by Charles Lamb. Lodged in Warwick University Library 1993.
15. Howard Barker. '49 Asides for a Tragic Theatre', *Guardian*, 10 February 1986. (Later published in *Arguments for a Theatre* by Howard Barker. Calder 1989.)
16. Howard Barker. Unpublished Interview with Charles Lamb. 23 April 1987. (See Note 14 above)
17. Ibid.
18. e.g. 'No Consistent Viewpoint' by Jonathan Hammond, *Plays and Players*, November 1975.

19. Robert Shaughnessy. 'Howard Barker, the Wrestling School, and the Cult of the Author', *New Theatre Quarterly*, Vol. V, No. 19, August 1989.
20. Ibid. p. 266.
21. *A Sense of Direction* by William Gaskill, Faber 1988. p. 49.
22. See Margaret Eddershaw's essay 'Acting Methods: Brecht and Stanislavsky', in *Brecht in Perspective*, ed. Bartrum and Waine, Longman 1982.
23. Stanislavsky's opening address to the assembled company of the first Moscow Art Theatre, 14 July 1898. Quoted in *Stanislavski: A Biography* by Jean Benedetti, Methuen 1988. p. 68.
24. Stanislavski: *A Biography*, Jean Benedetti. p. 46.
25. Brecht. 'Short Organum for the Theatre', in *Avant Garde Drama. A Casebook*, ed. Dukore and Gerould, Crowell 1976. p. 507
26. Ibid. pp. 508–509
27. Introduction to *The Fool and We Come to The River* by Edward Bond, Methuen 1976. p. xiii.
28. Howard Davies. 'Stock–Take at the Warehouse' in *Platform* 2, Summer 1980. p. 14.
29. Interview in *Plays and Players*, February 1979.
30. Danny Boyle. Talk at a day school on Howard Barker at Birbeck College, London, 10 December 1988.
31. *Arguments for a Theatre* by Howard Barker, 2nd edn. Manchester University Press 1993. pp. 67–70.
32. Ibid. p. 38.

CHAPTER 1

1. *The Worlds with The Activists Papers* by Edward Bond, Methuen 1980. p. 160.
2. 'The New Citröen' in *Mythologies* by Roland Barthes, Paladin 1976. p. 88.
3. *The Age of Enlightenment* by Isaiah Berlin, OUP 1979. p. 28.
4. *Phenomenology of Spirit* by G. W. F Hegel, tr. A. V. Miller, OUP 1977. p. 140.
5. *The Woman* by Edward Bond, from 'A Short Essay', Methuen 1979. p. 136.
6. *The Worlds with The Activists Papers*, Edward Bond. p. 91.

7. Jean Baudrillard. 'Symbolic Exchange and Death', in *Jean Baudrillard: Selected Writings*, Polity Press 1988. pp. 145–146.

8. Ibid. 'The Political Economy of the Sign'. p. 87.

9. J. K. Galbraith. *The New Industrial State*, Pelican 1969. p. 41.

10. *Jean Baudrillard: Selected Writings*. p. 73.

11. Jean–Francois Lyotard. From an interview 'On Theory' with Brigitte Devismes, printed in *Driftworks*, Semiotext (e) 1984. p. 29.

12. *Paraesthetics* by David Carroll, Methuen 1987. p. 188.

13. *The Postmodern Condition* by Jean–Francois Lyotard, Manchester University Press 1986. p. 74.

14. Ibid. p. 75.

15. David Edgar. 'Ten Years of Political Theatre — 1968–78', in *Theatre Quarterly*, No. 32, 1979. p. 27.

16. Ibid. p. 27.

17. See *Theatre at Work: The Story of the National Theatre's Production of Brecht's Galileo* by Jim Hiley, Routledge 1981.

18. See *Bertolt Brecht: Chaos According to Plan* by John Fuegi, CUP 1987. p. 84.

19. *The Life of Galileo* by Bertolt Brecht, tr. Willett, Methuen 1980. p. 129.

20. Ibid. p. 101.

21. *The Sleepwalkers* by Arthur Koestler, Pelican Books 1968. p. 484.

22. Cited in *The Sleepwalkers*, Arthur Koestler. p. 484.

23. Ibid. p. 487.

24. See *Galileo: Heretic* by Pietro Redondi, tr. Raymond Rosenthal, Allen Lane 1988.

25. *The Theatre of Bertolt Brecht* by John Willett, Eyre Methuen 1959. p. 170.

26. *Theory of the Modern Drama* by Peter Szondi. Polity Press 1987. p. 7.

27. Ibid. p. 7.

28. Ibid. p. 7.

29. Ibid. p. 8.

30. *Formalism and Marxism* by Tony Bennett, Methuen: New Accents 1979. p. 54.

31. 'Bond Unbound' by Martin Esslin, review of *Saved* in *Plays and Players*, April 1969.

32. Howard Barker. From an unpublished interview with Charles Lamb. 23 April 1987. (See Introduction, Note 14.)

33. *At the Royal Court — 25 Years of the English Stage Company*, ed. Richard Findlater, Amber Lane 1981. p. 109.

34. Aristotle. *Poetics* 3.

35. As defined in Liddell & Scott's *Greek–English Lexicon*, OUP.

36. Aristotle. *Poetics* 6.

37. Ibid. 26.
38. Ibid. 26.
39. *The Post Card* by Jacques Derrida, tr. Alan Bass, University of Chicago Press 1987. p. 123.
40. *The Dehumanisation of Art* by Ortega y Gasset, Princeton University Press 1969. p. 21.

CHAPTER 2

1. *Anti–Oedipus* by Deleuze and Guattari, tr. Hurley, Seem & Lane, Athlone 1984.
2. *Selected Writings*, Jean Baudrillard. p. 149.
3. *Being and Time* by Martin Heidegger, tr. Macquarrie & Robinson, Basil Blackwell 1980. §29. p. 52.
4. *Selected Writings*, Jean Baudrillard. p. 149.
5. Ibid. p. 162.
6. *Totality and Infinity* by Emmanuel Levinas, tr. Alphonso Lingis, Duquesne University Press, Pittsburgh 1969.
7. Emmanuel Levinas. 'Difficile Liberté', cited by Derrida in *Writing and Difference*, tr. Alan Bass, Routledge 1978. p. 91.
8. Ibid. p. 93.
9. *Collected Philosophical Papers* by Emmanuel Levinas, tr. Lingis, Martinus Nijhoff 1987. p. 41.
10. *The Possibilities* by Howard Barker, John Calder 1987. p. 56.
11. *Selected Writings*, Jean Baudrillard. p. 159.
12. Ibid. p. 158.
13. Ibid. p. 159.
14. Ibid. p. 161.
15. *Seduction* by Jean Baudrillard, tr. Brian Singer, Macmillan 1990. p. 69.
16. Ibid. pp. 69–70.
17. *Selected Writings*, Jean Baudrillard. p. 162.
18. Ibid. p. 163.
19. Howard Barker. From an Unpublished Interview with Charles Lamb, 23 April 1987. (See Introduction, Note 14.)
20. Ibid.
21. See *Arguments for a Theatre* by Howard Barker, John Calder 1989.
22. *Fatal Strategies* by Jean Baudrillard, Semiotext (e)/Pluto 1990. p. 156.

23. *The Bite of the Night* by Howard Barker, John Calder 1988. p. 4.
24. *The Last Supper* by Howard Barker, Calder 1988. p. 2.
25. Ibid. p. 2.
26. Ibid. p. 2.
27. *The Bite of the Night*. p. 3.
28. Ibid. pp. 3–4.
29. See for example '49 Asides for a Tragic Theatre' by Howard Barker, published in The Guardian, 10 February 1986. Also in *Arguments for a Theatre*.
30. 'The Street Scene: A Basic Model for an Epic Theatre' by Bertolt Brecht, tr. Willett in *The Theory of the Modern Stage,* ed. Bentley, Pelican 1968.
31. Barker: '49 Asides for a Tragic Theatre' in *Arguments for a Theatre*.
32. *Collected Philosophical Papers*, Emmanuel Levinas. p. 43.
33. *Fair Slaughter* by Howard Barker, Calder 1984. p. 35.
34. Ibid. p. 104.
35. *Crimes in Hot Countries* by Howard Barker, Calder 1984. p. 56.
36. *Selected Writings*, Jean Baudrillard. p. 161.
37. Ibid. p. 161.
38. *The Last Supper*. p. 56.
39. *Selected Writings*, Jean Baudrillard. p. 158.
40. *The Bite of the Night*, Act III Scene 2. From an unpublished pre–production text. Not included in the published version.
41. *The Power of the Dog* by Howard Barker, Calder 1985. p. 10.
42. Ibid. p. 17.
43. Ibid. p. 5.
44. *The Possibilities*. p. 70.
45. *Seduction*, Jean Baudrillard. p. 85.
46. *The Possibilities*. p. 71.
47. *Seduction*, Jean Baudrillard. p. 69.
48. *The Bite of the Night*. p. 59.
49. *The Europeans* by Howard Barker, John Calder 1990. pp. 4–5.
50. From 'Psychoanalysis and the Polis' by Julie Kristeva, in *The Kristeva Reader*, ed. Toril Moi, Basil Blackwell 1986. p. 315.
51. Ibid. pp. 315–316.
52. *North* by Louis Ferdinand Céline, tr. Ralph Manheim, The Bodley Head 1972. p. 1.
53. *The Kristeva Reader*. p. 317.
54. Howard Barker. Unpublished Interview with Charles Lamb, 23 April 1987. (See Chapter 1, Note 14.)
55. From 'La Parole Soufflée' in *Writing and Difference*, Jacques Derrida. p. 183.
56. *The Hang of the Gaol* by Howard Barker, Calder 1982. p. 19.

57. Ibid. pp. 12–13.
58. Ibid. p. 31.
59. Ibid. p. 80.
60. Ibid. p. 82.

CHAPTER 3

1. The Possibilities. Howard Barker. p. 57.
2. *Judith* by Howard Barker, John Calder 1990 (with *The Europeans*). p. 49. All further quotations in this chapter from *Judith* will indicate directly the page numbers of this edition.
3. *Selected Writings*, Jean Baudrillard, Polity 1988. p. 159.
4. *The Possibilities*, Howard Barker. p. 57.
5. *Seduction*, Jean Baudrillard. p. 74.
6. Ibid. p. 76.

CHAPTER 4

1. *The Castle* by Howard Barker, John Calder 1985. p. 19. All further quotations in this chapter from *The Castle* will indicate directly the page numbers of this edition.
2. 'Oppression, Resistance, and the Writer's Testament', Howard Barker interviewed by Finlay Donesky in *New Theatre Quarterly*, Vol. II, No. 8, November 1986. p. 338.
3. *Fatal Strategies*, Jean Baudrillard. p. 119.
4. Ibid. pp. 159–160.
5. Ibid. pp. 160–161
6. *The Architecture of Castles* by R. Allen Brown, Batsford 1984. p. 12.
7. Ibid. p. 9.
8. *The Anglo–Saxon Chronicle*, tr. & ed. G. N. Garmonsway, Everyman 1953. p. 264.
9. *Fatal Strategies*, Jean Baudrillard. p. 160.
10. Ibid. p. 160.
11. Republished in 1992 under the same title by Immel Publishing Ltd.

12. Ibid. p. 93.
13. Ibid. p. 97.
14. From *Howard Barker — Politics and Desire* by David Ian Rabey, Macmillan 1989. 'Appendix: Conversations'. p. 277.
15. Ibid. p. 277.
16. Ibid. p. 258.
17. Ibid. p. 258.
18. Ibid. p. 258.
19. Ibid. pp. 258–259.
20. *Towards a Poor Theatre* by Jerzy Grotowski, Methuen 1969. p. 205.
21. *Women's Review* No 2, 'The Castle': Interviews with Helen Carr. p. 33.
22. *The Bite of the Night*. p. 2.
23. *Theory of the Modern Drama*, Peter Szondi. p. 7.

SELECTIVE BIBLIOGRAPHY

1. BARKER

Almost all of the plays by Barker referred to in this study are published by John Calder. The exceptions are a number of unpublished early plays (see Production Chronology) and *Cheek* published by Eyre Methuen. Calder has also issued a book of criticism, *Arguments For a Theatre* (1989), and five books of poetry, *Don't Exaggerate* (1985), *The Breath of the Crowd* (1986), *Gary the Thief* (1987), *Lullabies for the Impatient* (1988), *The Ascent of Monte Grappa* (1991). *Arguments For a Theatre* was reissued in an expanded second edition by Manchester University Press (1993).

Other writings by Barker:

Barker, Howard, *Howard Barker on The Hang of The Gaol*, Warehouse Writers No. 1, RSC Warehouse, 1978.

Barker, Howard, Programme Notes on *The Loud Boy's Life*, RSC Warehouse, 1980.

Barker, Howard, 'The Possibilities.' Article on the current state of theatre in Britain, *Plays and Players*, March 1988.

2. CRITICAL AND OTHER WRITINGS ON BARKER.

Other published materials about Barker, or which refer to Barker are:

Ansorge, Peter, *Disrupting the Spectacle*, Pitman, London 1975.

Alexander, Bill 'Patriotic and Contentiously Left Wing' — Interview with Colin Chambers, *Plays and Players*, February 1979.

Bull, John, *New British Political Dramatists*, Macmillan, London 1984.

Carr, Helen, 'The Castle' — Discussion with Harriet Walter, Penny Downie and Kath Rogers, *Women's Review* No 2, 1986.

Chambers, Colin, *Other Spaces. New Theatre and the RSC*, Methuen, London 1980.

Davies, Howard, Interview, *Platform*, Summer 1980.

Donesky, Finlay, 'Oppression, Resistance and the Writer's Testament' — Interview with Howard Barker, *New Theatre Quarterly* Vol. II, No.8, November 1986.

Dunn, Tony, Ed. Gambit 41: *Howard Barker Special Issue*, John Calder, London 1984.

Dunn, Tony, 'The Play of Politics', *Theatre International*, Spring 1985.

Dunn, Tony, 'Writers of the Seventies', *Plays and Players*, June 1984.

Dunn, Tony, 'Howard Barker in the Pit', *Plays and Players*, October 1985.

Edgar, David, 'Ten Years of Political Theatre 1968–1978', *Theatre Quarterly*, Vol. 8, No. 32, 1979.

Grant, Steve, 'Barker's Bite', *Plays and Players*, December 1975.

Grant, Steve, 'Voicing the Protest: The New Writers', *Dreams and Deconstructions*, Ed. Craig. Amber Lane, England 1980.

Hiley, Jim, 'Language You Can Taste', (Article on *'Scenes from an Execution'*,) *Radio Times* 13–19 October 1984.

Hiley, Jim, 'Barker's Bite,' (Article on *'Pity in History'*,) *Radio Times* 29 June–5 July 1985.

Itzin, Catherine, *Stages in the Revolution*, Eyre Methuen, London 1980.

Lamb, Charles, 'Howard Barker's *"Crimes in Hot Countries"*: a Director's Approach', *Contradictory Theatres*, Ed. Leslie Bell, Theatre Action Press, England 1984.

Marks, Laurence, 'Off–beat Track', (Article based on Interview,) *Observer*, 21 February 1988.

Rabey, David Ian, *Howard Barker — Politics and Desire*, Macmillan, London,1989.

Rabey, David Ian, *British and Irish Political Drama in the Twentieth Century*, Macmillan, London 1986.

Rabey, David Ian, 'For the Absent Truth Erect: Impotence and Potency in Howard Barker's Recent Drama,' *Essays in Theatre/Etudes Theatrales* Vol. 10. No. 1, November 1991.

Rabey, David Ian, 'What do you see?: Howard Barker's *"The Europeans"*: A Director's Perpective', *Studies in Theatre Production* 6, December 1992.

Shaughnessy, Robert, 'Howard Barker, the Wrestling School, and the Cult of the Author', *New Theatre Quarterly* Vol. V, No. 19, August 1989.

Trussler, Simon, *New Theatre Voices of the Seventies*, Eyre Methuen, London 1981.

3. THEATRICAL/PERFORMANCE THEORY

Bartrum, Graham, and Waine, Anthony, Eds., *Brecht in Perspective,* Longman, London & New York 1982.

Benedetti, Jean, *Stanislavsky. A Biography*, Methuen, London 1988.

Bentley, Eric, Ed., *The Theory of the Modern Stage*, Pelican, England 1968.

Brecht, Bertolt, 'A Short Organum for the Theatre, (1948),' *Avant Garde Drama. A Casebook*, Ed. Dukore & Gerould. Crowell Casebooks, New York 1976.

Findlater, Richard, Ed. *At the Royal Court: 25 Years of the English Stage Company*, Amber Lane, England 1981.

Fuegi, John *Bertolt Brecht: Chaos According to Plan*, Cambridge University Press, London & New York 1987.

Gaskill, William, *A Sense of Direction*, Faber, London 1988.

Grotowski, Jerzy, *Towards a Poor Theatre*, Eyre Methuen, London 1969.

Stanislavsky, Konstantin, *My Life in Art*, Methuen, London 1980.

Szondi, Peter, *Theory of the Modern Drama*, Tr. & Ed. Hays, Polity Press, Cambridge 1987.

4. GENERAL THEORY/PHILOSOPHY

Barthes, Roland, *Mythologies*, Paladin, U. K. 1976.

Baudrillard, Jean, *Jean Baudrillard: Selected Writings*, Ed. Poster, Polity Press, Cambridge 1988.

Baudrillard, Jean, *Seduction*, Tr. Brian Singer, Macmillan, London 1990.

Baudrillard, Jean *Fatal Strategies*, Ed. Fleming, Semiotext(e)/Pluto, London & New York 1990.

Bennett, Tony, *Formalism and Marxism*, Methuen: New Accents, London & New York 1979.

Berlin, Isaiah, *The Age of Enlightenment*, Oxford University Press 1979.

Carroll, David, *Paraesthetics*, Methuen, New York & London 1987.

Deleuze, Gilles, and Guatteri, Felix, *Anti–Oedipus*, Tr. Hurley, Seem and Lane, Athlone, London 1984.

Derrida, Jacques, *The Post Card*, Tr. Alan Bass, University of Chicago Press, Chicago & London 1987.

Derrida, Jacques, *Writing and Difference*, Tr. Alan Bass, Routledge, London 1978.

Hegel, G. W. F., *Phenomenology of Spirit*, Tr. A. V. Miller, Oxford University Press 1977.

Heidegger, Martin, *Being and Time*, Tr. Macquarrie & Robinson, Blackwell, Oxford 1980.

Koestler, Arthur, *The Sleepwalkers*, Pelican Books, U. K. 1968.

Kristeva, Julie, *The Kristeva Reader*, Ed. Toril Moi, Blackwell, Oxford 1986.

Levinas, Emmanuel, *Totality and Infinity*, Tr. Alphonso Lingis, Duquesne University Press, Pittsburgh 1969.

Levinas, Emmanuel, *Collected Philosophical Papers*, Tr. Alphonso Lingis,

Martinus Nijhoff Publishers, Dordrecht, Netherlands 1987.
Lyotard, Jean–Francois, *Driftworks*, Semiotext(e), New York 1984.
Lyotard, Jean–Francois, *The Postmodern Condition: a Report on Knowledge*, Tr. Bennington and Massumi, Manchester University Press 1986.
Ortega Y Gasset, José, *The Dehumanization of Art*, Princeton University Press, 1968.

LIST OF THEATRE PREMIÈRES

(* indicates text unpublished. All others published by John Calder with the exception of *Cheek* by Eyre Methuen)

PLAY	DATE	VENUE/COMPANY	DIRECTOR
Cheek	11/9/70	Theatre Upstairs	William Gaskill
*No One Was Saved**	19/11/70	Theatre Upstairs	Pam Brighton
*Edward: The Final Days**	15/2/72	Open Space (L/T)	
*Faceache**	15/2/72	Recreation Ground	
*Alpha Alpha**	17/9/72	Open Space	
*Private Parts**	1972		
*Skipper, And My Sister And I**	12/3/73	Bush Theatre	
*Rule Britannia**	9/1/73	Open Space	
*Bang**	23/5/73	Open Space	
Claw	30/1/75	Open Space	Chris Parr
Stripwell	14/10/75	Royal Court	Chris Parr
Fair Slaughter	13/6/77	Royal Court	Stuart Burge
That Good Between Us	28/7/77	RSC Warehouse	Barry Kyle
The Love of a Good Man	19/10/78	Crucible Studio	David Leland
	13/11/79	Oxford Playhouse	Nicholas Kent
The Hang of The Gaol	15/12/78	RSC Warehouse	Bill Alexander
The Loud Boy's Life	26/2/80	RSC Warehouse	Howard Davies
Birth on a Hard Shoulder	8/11/80	Royal Dramatic Theatre Stockholm	Barbro Larsson
No End of Blame	11/2/81	Royal Court	Nicholas Kent
*The Poor Man's Friend**	1981	Colway Theatre Trust	Anne Jellicoe
Victory	17/2/83	Joint Stock/ Royal Court	Danny Boyle

Crimes in Hot Countries	15/3/83	Theatre Underground/ Essex University	Charles Lamb
	7/10/85	RSC Pit	Bill Alexander
A Passion in Six Days	7/10/83	Crucible Theatre Sheffield	Michael Boyd
The Power of The Dog	14/11/84	Joint Stock Hampstead	Kenny Ireland
The Castle	14/10/85	RSC Pit	Nick Hamm
Downchild	21/10/85	RSC Pit	Bill Alexander
Women Beware Women	1/2/86	Royal Court	William Gaskill
The Possibilities	23/2/88	Not The RSC/ Almeida	Ian McDiarmid
The Last Supper	8/3/88	Wrestling School/ Royal Court/ Leicester Haymarket	Kenny Ireland
The Bite of the Night	31/8/88	RSC Pit	Danny Boyle
Seven Lears	4/11/89	Wrestling School Leicester Haymarket	Kenny Ireland
Golgo	24/11/89	Wrestling School Leicester Haymarket	Nick Le Prevost
Scenes From an Execution	11/1/90	Almeida Theatre	Ian McDiarmid
A Hard Heart	3/3/92	Almeida Theatre	Ian McDiarmid
Terrible Mouth (Opera) Music by Nigel Osborne	10/7/92	Almeida Theatre	David Pountney
The Europeans	14/2/93	Wrestling School Leicester Haymarket	Kenny Ireland
Hated Nightfall	8/3/94	Wrestling School Dancehouse, Manchester	Howard Barker

INDEX

Other titles in the Contemporary Theatre Studies series:

This book is part of a series. The publisher will accept continuation orders which may be cancelled at any time and which provide for automatic billing and shipping of each title in the series upon publication. Please write for details.